THE POLITICS OF GENOCIDE

THE POLITICS OF GENOCIDE

by Edward S. Herman and David Peterson

MONTHLY REVIEW PRESS
New York

Library of Congress Cataloging-in-Publication Data

Herman, Edward S.

The politics of genocide / by Edward S. Herman and David Peterson.

   p. cm.

Includes bibliographical references and index.

ISBN 978-1-58367-212-9 (pbk.) — ISBN 978-1-58367-213-6 (cloth)

1. Genocide—History. I. Peterson, David, 1959– II. Title.

HV6322.7.H47 2010

364.15'1—dc22

                  2010004852

Monthly Review Press
146 West 29th Street, Suite 6W
New York, New York 10001

www.monthlyreview.org
www.MRzine.org

Contents

Reflections on *The Politics of Genocide* vii
Foreword by Noam Chomsky 7
Introduction... 13

CONSTRUCTIVE GENOCIDES 29
    1. The Iraq Sanctions-Regime Killings 29
    2. The Iraq Invasion-Occupation 33

NEFARIOUS GENOCIDES 39
    1. The Darfur Wars and Killings 39
    2. Bosnia and Herzegovina............................... 46
    3. Kosovo 49
    4. Rwanda and the Democratic Republic of Congo 51

SOME BENIGN BLOODBATHS 69
    1. Israel: Sabra and Shatila 69
    2. Israel: The Gaza Invasion of
       December 2008–January 2009........................ 73
    3. Croatia's Operation Storm 81
    4. Dasht-e-Leili (Afghanistan) 84
    5. Turkey's Kurds vs. Iraq's Kurds 87
    6. Indonesia and East Timor—Liquiçá 89
    7. El Salvador and Guatemala........................... 91

MYTHICAL BLOODBATHS 95
    Račak 95

Concluding Note.. 103
Notes... 113
Index... 151

Reflections on
The Politics of Genocide

Edward S. Herman and David Peterson

Almost immediately after we submitted *The Politics of Genocide* to Monthly Review Press in late March 2009, a series of events unfolded that confirmed our analysis of the political basis of the use versus non-use of the words "genocide" and "massacre" to describe different theaters of atrocity. Now, writing some two-and-one-half years later, we can state without exaggeration that our critique was robust: It fits well not only with how the politics of "genocide" has continued to play out, but also with how the same political factors extend to a much wider range of events and the treatment they receive by establishment institutions, including the media, intellectuals, and activists deeply integrated into the U.S. power structure.[1]

REGIME CHANGE IN LIBYA

"I reassure everyone that this story has ended and this book has closed," a military spokesman for Libya's National Transitional Council announced over al-Jazeera TV. "Muammar Gaddafi has been killed," NTC interim prime minister Mahmoud Jibril told a news conference in Tripoli the same day. Gaddafi was the "first of the autocrats to be killed in the Arab Spring uprisings," as the *New York Times* described the event—and in UN Secretary-General Ban Ki-Moon's words, an "historic moment," the "end of the 42-year reign of the Gaddafi regime." "The war's over," the French philosopher Bernard-Henri Lévy commented. "The bloodbath is over."[2]

Muammar Gaddafi's October 20, 2011, death at the hands of National Transitional Council (NTC) fighters after the convoy of vehicles in which he was traveling had been nearly incinerated by U.S. Predator missiles outside his birthplace of Sirte, and the deaths of an unknown number of Gaddafi loyalists and civilians in Sirte and in the many other Libyan cities where the resistance to the NTC and NATO forces lasted the longest, came almost seven months to the day after the U.S. military launched its first cruise missile and bombing attacks on the Gaddafi regime (March 19), in direct violation of the UN Security Council resolutions that Washington and its allies in Paris and London and Brussels repeatedly cited to justify their attack on Libya.[3] "In this particular country—Libya—at this particular moment, we were faced with the prospect of violence on a horrific scale," U.S. President Barack Obama explained at the National Defense University in Washington on March 28. "Some nations may be able to turn a blind eye to atrocities in other countries," he continued. But the "United States of America is different. And as President, I refused to wait for the images of slaughter and mass graves before taking action."[4]

Why and according to which—or whose—moral metric NATO's participation in the next seven months of armed conflict and *actual* bloodbaths, including the NTC's targeting of black African workers,[5] which swept across Libya first from the east and then also from the west toward Tripoli, Misrata, Bani Walid, and ultimately Sirte, was to be preferred to a *potential* bloodbath that Gaddafi's forces allegedly had in store back in late March for his opposition in Benghazi, no one has ever explained. As Jean Bricmont and Diana Johnstone noted shortly before Gaddafi fled Tripoli in August: "The activists who in March insisted that 'we must do something' to stop a hypothetical massacre are doing nothing today to stop a massacre that is not hypothetical but real and visible, and carried out by those who 'did something.'"[6] Such was NATO's first-ever application of the Responsibility to Protect doctrine,[7] an advance, it is alleged, over the "illegal but legitimate" formula used in defense of NATO's earlier "humanitarian intervention" in Kosovo in 1999.[8] The "bloodbath" that Bernard-Henri Lévy mentioned may be over, but only because this was a NATO-instigated bloodbath from start to finish.

Rather than the "protection of civilians" called for by UN Security Council Resolution 1973 (March 17),[9] the 2011 war over Libya was a case of imperial warmaking in the real world. It took only seven days after the regime responded to the first anti-Gaddafi protests in Benghazi (February 15) for the regime to wind up before the UN Security Council (February 22), with much rhetoric about Libya's need to "meet its responsibility to protect its population" and to "hold to account those responsible for attacks . . . on civilians."[10] And it took only four more days for the council to adopt its first resolution against the regime (February 26), an act that gravely misrepresented the regime's response to the rapid escalation of the foreign-sponsored insurgency[11] as nothing but a straightforward "repression of peaceful demonstrators" and "incitement to hostility and violence against the civilian population."[12] UNSC Resolution 1970 included a referral of the "situation" in Libya to the prosecutor of the International Criminal Court, while immunizing the non-Libyan persons of any state "not a party to the Rome Statute" from the ICC's jurisdiction in this particular case—a clear U.S. demand, in keeping with the U.S. practice of rejecting international law of any kind that might apply to its own personnel, and a harbinger of what kind of brutal military enforcement lay ahead.[13]

Five days later (March 3), ICC prosecutor Luis Moreno-Ocampo announced that his examination of the information then available warranted his opening an investigation of the Gaddafi regime. "There will be no impunity in Libya," he said at The Hague. "No one has authority to attack and massacre civilians."[14] Later, in his first report to the Security Council, Moreno-Ocampo explained that the "situation in Libya . . . clearly meets the threshold of gravity required by the ICC Statute," and "there were no substantial reasons to believe that the investigation would not serve the interests of justice."[15] As we pointed out in *The Politics of Genocide*, when in February 2006 Moreno-Ocampo declined to open an investigation into atrocities committed by the United States and its allies during their war and occupation of Iraq, he used much the same language as he did for the Gaddafi regime, but he reversed his conclusion, as well as the principle that his office would uphold: U.S. atrocities in Iraq "did not appear to meet the required threshold of the Statute," he said.[16] This was nearly three years into an illegal war of aggression against a sovereign member of the United Nations, with a massive death toll and a sustained refugee crisis running into several million persons; and it was sixteen years into the U.S. and U.K. economic, political, and military siege of an entire country of more than twenty million persons. But none of this mattered. Some of the ICC Prosecutor's thresholds can be readily met, and others never. Such is "international justice" at the start of the twenty-first century.

When this whole multilateral phalanx oriented around U.S. power—including NATO's leadership, the Security Council, the Secretary-General, the UN Human Rights Council, the International Criminal Court, non-governmental human rights organizations, media, intellectuals, and activists—mobilized against the Gaddafi regime in the second half of February 2011, this enabled the U.S.-led NATO powers to launch a war that never had any real purpose other than to overthrow the regime. In fact, when Russia's UN ambassador, Vitaly Churkin, explained

his country's reasons for vetoing a draft Security Council resolution in early October 2011 that would have imposed sanctions on
the al-Assad regime for the violent conflict that it was waging
inside Syria, Churkin stated that the "situation in Syria cannot be
considered in the Council separately from the Libyan experience." Churkin continued:

> The international community is alarmed by statements that
> compliance with Security Council resolutions on Libya in the
> NATO interpretation is a model for the future actions of
> NATO in implementing the responsibility to protect. It is easy
> to see that today's "Unified Protector" model could happen in
> Syria. . . . For us, Members of the United Nations, including in
> terms of a precedent, it is very important to know how the
> [Libyan] resolution was implemented and how a Security
> Council resolution turned into its opposite. . . . The demand for
> a quick ceasefire turned into a full-fledged civil war, the human-
> itarian, social, economic and military consequences of which
> transcend Libyan borders. The situation in connection with the
> no-fly zone has morphed into the bombing of oil refineries, tel-
> evision stations and other civilian sites. The arms embargo has
> morphed into a naval blockade in western Libya, including a
> blockade of humanitarian goods. Today the tragedy of
> Benghazi has spread to other western Libyan towns—Sirte and
> Bani Walid. These types of models should be excluded from
> global practices once and for all.[17]

But in February–March 2011, with the U.S., French, and British
powers eager to drive the Gaddafi regime from power, no amount
of actual or reported violence was going to be too small to deter
these engaged humanitarians from the resort to war, or too low
not to meet Moreno-Ocampo's anti-Gaddafi threshold. As
Samantha Power, the National Security Council's senior director
for multilateral affairs and human rights, noted in late February:

This is already breaking with precedent in many important ways. Normally, when a government is targeting its own people, it takes longer for the United States to open its tool box and deploy tools that have bite. We have already seen a preparedness to scale the ladder of escalation.[18]

THE SRI LANKA EXEMPTION

Yet, in one enlightening case where this ladder of escalation was never scaled, a massively violent final assault had been launched by the Sri Lankan government against the Liberation Tigers of Tamil Eelam (LTTE) and the minority Tamil population of the Vanni region in the north of this island country.[19] By early 2009, an estimated 330,000 civilians were pinned down inside increasingly smaller government-declared "no-fire zones" north of the city of Mullaittivu, along the Bay of Bengal coastline; these civilian concentrations shrank from twenty-two square miles, to eight, to one square mile by May, as each of these "no-fire zones" came under unrelenting aerial and artillery bombardment by the Sri Lankan Army, with massive civilian casualties.[20] Although the 2011 Report of the Secretary-General's Panel of Experts on Accountability in Sri Lanka noted that "there is still no reliable figure for civilian deaths," it added that "multiple sources of information indicate that a range of up to 40,000 civilian deaths cannot be ruled out at this stage."[21]

Throughout the period from January through May 2009 appeals were made to both parties to the conflict, to the United Nations, and to interested states to invoke the R2P doctrine and provide some relief to a civilian population caught between the Sri Lankan Army and what was left of the armed forces of the LTTE, which the army offensive was systematically destroying. At a January 31 press conference in nearby Chennai India, the Tamil-related People's Union for Civil Liberties lamented that the "international community appears to have decided to play mute spectators to the dreadful drama of death and destruction that has befallen the Tamils of northern Sri Lanka," and called upon the "United Nations to invoke the *doctrine of 'Responsibility to Protect'* and to proactively intervene in the Sri Lankan crisis on an emergency basis to prevent further aggravation of the humanitarian crisis."[22] The Norwegian government, for many years the lead negotiator between the LTTE and the Sri Lankan government, also "condemn[ed] the current conduct of hostilities in Sri Lanka causing unacceptable suffering to civilians in the country," and reminded the Sri Lankan government and the LTTE that they "both . . . have a responsibility to protect the civilian population and prevent civilian deaths."[23]

But neither the United Nations nor any coalition of states took up these calls during the crucial months of January–May 2009, and the Security Council has never debated, let alone adopted, a resolution that would refer these atrocities against the Tamil civilians to the prosecutor at the International Criminal Court to open an investigation. In the UN Panel of Experts' report there is no discussion of the R2P doctrine in the context of Sri Lanka's bloody 2008–2009 defeat of the LTTE and the massive civilian deaths and crimes that accompanied the action. Nor did the panel recommend that the UN Security Council refer the matter to the ICC to open an investigation into the Sri Lankan government's termination of the three-decade-long LTTE insurgency on behalf of a separate Tamil state, even though the panel's report makes it clear that "tens of thousands lost their lives from January to May 2009" as the government transformed its "no-fire zones" into what were essentially anti-Tamil "free-fire" zones.

Thus, although a state's "unwillingness or inability genuinely to carry out the investigation" into its own crimes counts under the ICC's Rome Statute as one of the triggers for action by the prosecutor to open an investigation into possible crimes, and though the

UN Panel of Experts' opinion is that the "Government of Sri Lanka has not discharged its responsibilities to conduct a genuine investigation, nor has it shown signs of an intention to do so"—Sri Lanka remains to this day *ICC-free*, just as it remained *R2P-free* throughout the bloodiest of its army's attack on the Tamil civilian population of the Vanni region.[24] Indeed, as late as September 2011, more than two years after the end of the major bloodbaths in Sri Lanka, an Amnesty International report criticized Secretary-General Ban Ki-moon for his failure to "establish an independent international accountability mechanism" into likely crimes under humanitarian and human rights laws, on the false pretense that "he awaited authorization from another UN body, such as the Security Council or the Human Rights Council." But, Amnesty International added, Ban had not yet even "officially submitted the Panel's report to the Human Rights Council."[25]

LIBYA VERSUS SRI LANKA

The contrast between the systematic and long-standing impunity enjoyed by the Sri Lankan regime, despite its massive assault on the Tamil population in 2008–2009, and Ban's and the UN High Commissioner for Human Rights Navi Pillay's quick condemnation of the Gaddafi regime within the first week to ten days of its response to a foreign-sponsored insurgency in eastern Libya, along with Moreno-Ocampo's equally quick investigation of the Gaddafi regime and eventual securing of arrest warrants for Muammar Gaddafi, his son, Saif, and his brother-in-law, Abdullah Al-Senussi,[26] is breathtaking. Database searches of the same wire-service and newspaper universe for mentions of "Sri Lanka" or "Libya" in relation to "responsibility to protect" (and similar terms, such as "R2P") find that the R2P doctrine was mentioned roughly once in relation to Sri Lanka for every fifteen times it was mentioned in relation to Libya.[27] Such differences in word usage by the establishment media reflected the differences in political agendas at the center of global power, but clearly had nothing to do with concerns for real-world violence against civilians, or the protection of civilians from harm. As we have indicated, the level of violence was far greater against the Tamils of northern Sri Lanka (September 2008–May 2009) than was the violence directed against Libyans in the east through the dates of the two UN Security Council resolutions (February 26 and March 17, 2011). Moreover, the level of the Gaddafi regime's violence against Libyans was much lower prior to the start of the U.S., French, and U.K. attack on March 19, 2011, than it became after March 19. Also, the Gaddafi regime's violence was much lower overall than was the violence and military firepower unleashed by the NATO powers and the fighters with their National Transitional Council client against the regime in the seven months following March 19—or else the Gaddafi regime might still rule in Tripoli.

The real politics at work here was that Muammar Gaddafi, although having made strong accommodation with the West in recent years (notably, Gaddafi's abandonment of Libya's nuclear weapons program in December 2003, a lesson to all would-be proliferators not on the best of terms with the United States[28]), remained an independent force, organizing African Union countries to resist Western domination, and encouraging China to partner with it in the ongoing development of Libya's energy resources. What's more, as recently as the summer of 2009, Gaddafi had used his chairmanship of the African Union to lobby fellow AU members against the ICC for what an earlier AU declaration had called the ICC's "misuse of indictments against African leaders."[29] One of the decisions adopted by the AU in Gaddafi's hometown of Sirte in 2009 stated that "AU Member States shall not cooperate" with the ICC's arrest warrant for Sudan's president Omar El Bashir.[30] In consequence, when the initial protests of the "Arab Spring" provided the Western Great

Powers with a pretext to carry out regime change in Libya under the cover of rescuing a popular "pro-democracy" uprising from destruction by the forces of its own government, they actively encouraged, organized, armed, and propagandized on behalf of the anti-Gaddafi insurgency—and with their massive air and logistical support overthrew the Gaddafi regime in little more than half a year.

But the Western powers' relationship with Sri Lanka was radically different. The United States and its allies maintained steadily friendly relations with the majority Sinhalese regime in Colombo, and hoped to mobilize it as a southeast Asian arm of NATO. The United States alone has given some $2 billion in aid money to Sri Lanka, helped to train its military, and maintains an International Broadcast Bureau radio transmitting facility there (formerly Voice of America). In its 2011 Background Note on Sri Lanka, the U.S. Department of State described the regime of President Mahinda Rajapaksa (November 2005–) as "strongly democratic," among other superlatives, and singled out the Rajapaksa regime's "moderate nonaligned foreign policy" and constructive role in having defeated the "terrorist activities" of the LTTE.[31]

What followed on the international stage from these political alignments between Sri Lanka and Libya and the United States and its allies was this: Whereas the Gaddafi regime's initial military response to the insurgency in the east constituted a "nefarious" bloodbath and even a looming "genocide," and elicited not only indignant charges and threats but also open superpower warfare against it, the Rajapaksa regime's systematic and sustained destruction of the LTTE insurgency along with tens of thousands of Tamil civilians was "benign," and incapable of rising to the threshold that would activate the R2P contingents in the Security Council, or the ICC prosecutor. Gaddafi's Libya would be quickly condemned and bombed relentlessly, until it was destroyed; Rajapaksa's Sri Lanka would be politely requested by the U.S. State Department to carry out its own "credible domestic investigation" into its alleged war crimes, and then threatened with possible U.S. support for at least some scrutiny, which is "exactly the kind of international action that the Sri Lankans say they don't want."[32] For his part, Ban Ki-Moon would travel to Colombo only days after the Sri Lanka Army's final assault on the Tamil, where he expressed his pleasure at the Rajapaksa regime's "commitment to the promotion and protection of human rights" and an "accountability process for addressing violations of international humanitarian and human rights law"—that is, for the regime's promise to investigate itself![33] No threats were issued by these parties beyond that of brutal international scrutiny, certainly not action to protect civilians.

CONCLUDING NOTE

It is vital for a world ruled by force that those military powers that possess the greatest means of violence also possess a vast repertoire of pseudo-justifications upon which they can draw whenever they need to deny the barbarity of their regular practices.

"The mission of the coalition led by France was to prevent the massacre of civilians in the Libyan cities," the engaged "humanitarian" warrior Bernard-Henri Lévy told Reuters Television on the day Muammar Gaddafi was captured and executed. "In consequence it was to reduce, to prevent him from being harmful, to capture and arrest the man who was the organizer of this massacre of civilians. Today that's been done."[34] In reality, what the Western powers did was to devastate the country, kill and displace a very large number of civilians, and leave Libya a leaderless and disorganized country—a "failed state."

In the two cases we have compared here, as in scores of others,[35] the establishment Western media observe what we may call a *State Department-needs model*.[36] In this model, whereas the leaders of the targeted state are menacing or simply evil, and will be demonized, the leaders in allied or client states will at worst be chided for regrettable indiscretions, their misdeeds ignored, downplayed, or placed in a context of extenuating circumstances.

That substantial segments of the Left in the United States, France, and Britain also wound up closely following this pattern in treating the relevant developments in Libya and Sri Lanka was troubling, as any resistance to the imperial powers requires a well-informed, critical opposition by left intellectuals, left media, and Left activists living and working within these powers. But what we have witnessed instead over the past two-and-one-half years was a disarming of the Left, with the Left's attention, passions, and moral indignation channeled in accord with Western imperial demands.

Such channeling already was dramatically evident in the wars that dismantled Yugoslavia (1991–) and led to the U.S. and NATO conquest by force of the Serbian province of Kosovo (1999–), with the liberal and a substantial segment of the left intellectual establishment accepting that these were cases of "humanitarian intervention" (if too late and insufficiently violent). Over the past two decades, many left-liberal spokespersons climbed aboard various other bandwagons, all of which aligned with U.S. policy from Afghanistan to Iraq to Darfur. But many of these same left-liberal spokespersons have remained silent on the repression of the popular forces in post-coup Honduras (June 28, 2009–),[37] just as they have on the ongoing disclosures that enlarged the huge backlog of evidence implicating Rwanda's dictator, Paul Kagame, and his Rwandan Patriotic Front's two-decade-long bloodbaths, first in seizing state power within Rwanda (1990–1994), and then across the Democratic Republic of Congo (1996–).[38]

In short, the politics of genocide continues without mitigation in the age of the alleged rise of R2P and a new world order oriented around human rights and the fabled end to impunity. The politically based double standard remains intact and solid.

Notes

1. For our discussion of the analytic model that we used throughout *The Politics of Genocide*, see our Introduction, pp. 15–17. As we describe our basic approach in our Concluding Note (p. 103): The whole structure of the Western establishment's representation of world events replicates to a remarkable degree a dichotomous treatment that is in strict accord with Western power and policy preferences, and that can be expressed by two general rules: (1) When we ourselves commit mass-atrocity crimes, the atrocities are *constructive*, our victims are *unworthy* of our attention and indignation, and never suffer "genocide" at our hands. (2) When the perpetrator of mass-atrocity crimes is our enemy or a state targeted by us for destabilization and attack, the converse is true. Then the atrocities are *nefarious* and their victims *worthy* of our focus, sympathy, public displays of solidarity, and calls for inquiry and punishment.

2. In Christopher Gillette and Kim Gamel, "Gadhafi, Libya's leader for 42 years until ousted by his people, killed as hometown falls," Associated Press, October 20, 2011; Kareem Fahim et al., "Qaddafi, Seized by Foes, Meets a Violent End," *New York Times*, October 21, 2011; "As Libya Closes 'Painful, Tragic Chapter', Secretary-General Pays Tribute to Libyan People's Courage" (SG/SM/13891), UN Department of Public Information, October 20, 2011; and "Key Sarkozy Libya advisor says Gadhafi dictatorship and war are now over," Reuters Television, October 20, 2011.

3. See UN Security Council Resolution 1970, February 26, 2011; and UN Security Council Resolution 1973, March 17, 2011.

4. Barack Obama, "Remarks by the President in Address to the Nation on Libya," National Defense University, Washington, D.C., White House Office of the Press Secretary, March 28, 2011.

5. Many accounts have reported the rise of anti-black sentiment and violence against black persons inside Libyan national territory since late February 2011. See, for example, Maximilian Forte, "The War in Libya: Race, 'Humanitarianism', and the Media," *MRZine*, April 20, 2011; Kim Sengupta, "Rebels Settle Scores in Libyan Capital," *The Independent*, August 27, 2011; David D. Kirkpatrick, "Libyans Turn Wrath on Dark-Skinned Migrants," *New York Times*, September 5, 2011; Simba Russeau, "Hatred Divides Libya after Gaddafi," Inter Press Service, October 24, 2011; and Michael McGehee, "'Free' Libya: The rise of NATO's racist, executing liberators," *ZNet* Blogs, October 24, 2011.—Here we add that the wrath, not of "Libyans" *per se*, but of the fighters with the anti-Gaddafi insurgency, had been turned against blacks living and working in Libya from the very start of the war in February.

6. Jean Bricmont and Diana Johnstone, "Who Will Save Libya from Its Western Saviours?" *CounterPunch*, August 16, 2011. Also see Marinella Correggia, "Urgent Questions to NATO on Libya," *Pravda-English*, September 13, 2011; Pierre Lévy, "Libya: NATO provides the bombs; The French 'left' provides the ideology," Trans. Diana Johnstone, *MRZine*, October 5, 2011; and Seumus Milne, "If the Libyan war was about saving lives, it was a catastrophic failure," *The Guardian*, October 27, 2011.

7. See the 2005 World Summit Outcome document (A/RES/60/1), UN General Assembly, September 15, 2005, para. 138–139.

8. See Richard Goldstone et al., *The Kosovo Report: Conflict, International Response, Lessons Learned, Independent International Commission on Kosovo* (New York: Oxford University Press, 2001). The exact passage reads: "The Commission concludes that the NATO military intervention was illegal but legitimate. It was illegal because it did not receive prior approval from the United Nations Security Council. However, the Commission considers that the intervention was justified because all diplomatic avenues had been exhausted and because the intervention had the effect of liberating the majority population of Kosovo from a long period of oppression under Serbian rule" (p. 4).

9. See UNSC Resolution 1973, para. 4–5. Paragraph 4 authorized "Member States . . . to take all necessary measures . . . to protect civilians and civilian populated areas under threat of attack in the Libyan Arab Jamahiriya, including Benghazi, while excluding a foreign occu-

pation force of any form on any part of Libyan territory. . . . " But 1973 manifestly did not authorize any state to arm and organize and direct the insurgency, as the United States, France, and Britain did. Nor did 1973 authorize any state or regional organization such as NATO to provide all the necessary aerial support that the insurgency would require to overthrow the legitimate government of Libya.

10. "Security Council Press Statement on Libya" (SC/10180), UN Department of Public Information, February 22, 2011. Note that the council's February 22 session was *closed*, and no meeting record has been published.

11. Many news reports have placed combinations of U.S., French, and British "special forces" inside Libyan national territory by late February 2011. See, for example, "U.S. military advisers in Cyrenaica," *DEBKAfile* Special Report, February 25, 2011, reporting "hundreds" of "military advisers," making the operation the "first time America and Europe have intervened militarily in any of the popular upheavals rolling through the Middle East. . . ." Also see Mark Hosenball, "Obama authorizes secret help for Libya rebels," Reuters, March 30, 2011; Pauline Jelinek, "U.S. says no American 'boots' on the ground in Libya, but it's fancy footwork: The CIA is there," Associated Press, March 31, 2011; Nicholas Watt and Paul Harris, "Cameron agrees with U.S. on legality of arming rebels," *The Guardian*, March 31, 2011; Mark Mazzetti and Eric Schmitt, "Top Libyan Official Defects; Rebels Are Retreating: C.I.A. Spies Aiding Airstrikes and Assessing Qaddafi's Foes," *New York Times*, March 31, 2011; Karen DeYoung and Greg Miller, "CIA at work inside Libya," *Washington Post*, March 31, 2011.

12. UNSC Resolution 1970, p. 1.

13. See UNSC Resolution 1970, para. 6.

14. "International Criminal Court investigates Libya violence in response to UN request," UN News Center, March 3, 2011.

15. *First Report of the Prosecutor of the International Criminal Court to the UN Security Council Pursuant to UNSCR 1970 (2011)*, Office of the Prosecutor, International Criminal Court, May 4, 2011, para. 16, para. 21.

16. See *The Politics of Genocide*, pp. 104–109.

17. "The situation in the Middle East" (S/PV.6627), UN Security Council, October 4, 2011, pp. 3–5; here p. 4.

18. In Scott Wilson, "Threat to Americans guided restrained Libya response," *Washington Post*, February 27, 2011.

19. The armed insurgency by the Liberation Tigers of Tamil Eelam (LTTE) dates as far back as 1983, but the final, methodical, well-

planned, and successful destruction of the insurgency that was conducted by the regime of Sri Lankan president Mahinda Rajapaksa is
conventionally dated from January 2008 on, when the Rajapaksa
regime unilaterally terminated an internationally mediated ceasefire
agreement with the LTTE, and the European-staffed Sri Lanka
Monitoring Mission, which had documented ceasefire violations,
withdrew its monitors. The Sri Lankan Army's final offensive
stretched from September 2008 through May 19, 2009, when, in a televised, ceremonial news conference in Colombo, the Sri Lanka
defense secretary (and brother to the president), Gotabhaya
Rajapakse, and the army chief-of-staff, Lieut.-Gen. Sarath Fonseka,
declared the military offensive against the LTTE officially ended:
"Now the entire country is declared rid of terrorism," Fonseka said.

20.   See *Report to Congress on Incidents during the Recent Conflict in Sri
       Lanka*, U.S. Department of State, 2009, "Map of the area," p. 2, n. 1.
21.   Marzuki Darusman et al., *Report of the Secretary-General's Panel of
       Experts on Accountability in Sri Lanka*, March 31, 2011, para.
       132–137; here para. 137. The report also states that "The [UN's]
       decision not to provide specific figures made the issue of civilian casu-
       alties less newsworthy," and adds that "Some have criticized the fail-
       ure of the United Nations to present figures publicly as events were
       unfolding, citing it as excessively cautious in comparison with other
       conflict situations" (para. 136).
22.   "Humanitarian Crisis in northern Sri Lanka," People's Union for Civil
       Liberties—Tamil, Nadu and Puducherry, Press Statement, emphasis
       in original, January 31, 2011.
23.   "The Norwegian Government: Unacceptable suffering among civil-
       ians in Sri Lanka" (09/09), Norwegian Ministry of Foreign Affairs,
       January 27, 2009.
24.   See Rome Statute of the International Criminal Court, Article 18(3).
       Sri Lanka is not a signatory to the Rome Statute, and under the statute
       it therefore would require a referral by the Security Council before the
       prosecutor could agree to open an investigation. Also see Darusman
       et al., "Executive Summary," p. iii and para. 441.
25.   Sri Lanka: When Will They Get Justice? Failures of Sri Lanka's
       Lessons Learnt and Reconciliation Commission (ASA 37/008/
       2011), Amnesty International, September 7, 2011, p. 8. As AI con-
       cludes: "Given Sri Lanka's long history of failed commissions of
       inquiry, ... Amnesty International does not consider that the [official]
       LLRC will ever deliver justice, truth and full reparations to Sri Lankan
       victims of human rights violations. The LLRC was never an appropri-
       ate mechanism for investigating crimes of the magnitude alleged to

have occurred in the final days of Sri Lanka's armed conflict.... The UN has a responsibility to investigate allegations of crimes under international law without delay ... " ("The Need for an Independent Investigation," p. 58).

26. See Luis Moreno-Ocampo, *Prosecutor's Application Pursuant to Article 58 as to Muammar Mohammed Abu Minyar Gaddafi, Sair Al-Islam Gaddafi and Abdullah Al-Senussi* (ICC-01-11), International Criminal Court, May 16, 2011; and for the ICC's acceptance of these requests, see Judge Sanji Mmasenono Monageng et al., Decision on *"Prosecutor's Application Pursuant to Article 58 as to Muammar Mohammed Abu Minyar Gaddafi, Sair Al-Islam Gaddafi and Abdullah Al-Senussi"* (ICC-01-11), International Criminal Court, June 27, 2011.

27. Factiva database searches carried out under the "Wires" (*twir*) and "Newspapers: All" (*tnwp*) categories on October 20, 2011. The exact search parameters were as follows: For Sri Lanka: *rst=(twir* or *tnwp)* and *(responsibility to protect* or *R2P* or *RtoP)* for the 243-day time period October 1, 2008, through May 31, 2009; and for Libya: *rst=(twir* or *tnwp)* and *(responsibility to protect* or *R2P* or *RtoP)* for the 243-day period from February 15, 2001, through October 15, 2011. The results were: For Sri Lanka: 150; for Libya: 1,470.

28. See, for example, Diederik Vandewalle, "The origins and parameters of Libya's bold about-face," *The Daily Star*, March 22, 2004; Nicholas Watt, "UK firms line up big Libya deals: Blair praises Gadafy's courage ahead of historic visit," *The Guardian*, March 25, 2004; Simon Tisdall, "Talk, talk or bomb, bomb?" *The Guardian*, March 25, 2004.

29. *Communiqué of the 142nd Meeting of the Peace and Security Council* (PSC/MIN/Comm(CXLII)), African Union, Addis Ababa, July 21, 2008, para. 3.

30. *Decision on the Meeting of African States Parties to the Rome Statute of the International Criminal Court* (Assembly/AU/Dec.245(XIII)), African Union, Sirte, July 3, 2009, para. 10.

31. "Background Note: Sri Lanka," U.S. Department of State, April 6, 2011.

32. Daya Gamage, "U.S. State Department threatens Sri Lanka could face 'Global Probe,' that 'they say they didn't want'," *Asia Tribune*, August 10, 2011.

33. "Durable political solution key to development in post-conflict Sri Lanka—Ban," UN News Center, May 24, 2009.

34. "Key Sarkozy Libya advisor says Gadhafi dictatorship and war are now over," Reuters Television, October 20, 2011.

35. See, for example, Edward S. Herman and David Peterson, "Legitimizing versus Delegitimizing Elections: Honduras and Iran,"

in Gerald Sussman, ed., *The Propaganda Society: Promotional Culture and Politics in Global Context* (New York: Peter Lang, 2011), pp. 193–212.

36. In this phrase, "State Department" is to be taken as a metonym for the totality of the U.S. and allied foreign-policy establishment, along with the recognition that if the United States doesn't throw the massive weight of its military, political, and cultural resources behind a policy, the policy isn't likely to go very far within the so-called "international community." Thus when this interrelated foreign policy establishment with Washington at its center and NATO and beyond as its umbrella coalesces against an official "enemy" regime and targets it with destabilization and a demonization campaign, a State Department-needs model suggests that many suppliers will provide the policymakers with material acts of destabilization (isolation, sanctions, sponsorship of terrorism and groups with the capacity to pressure and discredit the government, all the way to military intervention and regime change) as well as propagandistic acts of delegitimation and negative publicity campaigns against the regime. In other words, what the U.S. foreign policy establishment and its allies demand, governments, organizations, and individuals rush in to supply. With the current state of information technology, the number of providers able to supply propaganda and to participate in negative publicity campaigns against a demonized "enemy" has grown exponentially.

37. See Edward S. Herman and David Peterson, "Iran and Honduras in the Propaganda System, Part 1: Neda Agha-Soltan versus Isis Obed Murillo," *MRZine*, October 5, 2010; and Edward S. Herman and David Peterson, "Iran and Honduras in the Propaganda System, Part 2: The 2009 Iranian and Honduran Elections," *MRZine*, October 24, 2010.

38. See *Democratic Republic of Congo, 1993–2003: Report of the Mapping Exercise documenting the most serious violations of human rights and international humanitarian law committed within the territory of the Democratic Republic of the Congo between March 1993 and June 2003*, United Nations Office of the High Commissioner for Human Rights, August 2010. Also see Edward S. Herman and David Peterson, "Paul Kagame: 'Our Kind of Guy'," ZNet, October 5, 2010.

Foreword
by Noam Chomsky

Perhaps the most shattering lesson from this powerful inquiry is that the end of the Cold War opened the way to an era of virtual Holocaust denial. As the authors put it, more temperately, "[d]uring the past several decades, the word 'genocide' has increased in frequency of use and recklessness of application, so much so that the crime of the 20th Century for which the term originally was coined often appears debased." Current usage, they show, is an insult to the memory of victims of the Nazis.

It may be useful, however, to recall that the practices are deeply rooted in prevailing intellectual culture, so much so that they will not be easy to eradicate. We can see this by considering the most unambiguous cases of genocide and cases in which the word has been debased, those in which the crime is acknowledged by the perpetrators, and passed over as insignificant or even denied in retrospect by the beneficiaries, right to the present.

Settler colonialism, commonly the most vicious form of imperial conquest, provides striking illustrations. The English colonists in North America had no doubts about what they were doing. Revolutionary War hero General Henry Knox, the first

Secretary of War in the newly liberated American colonies, described "the utter extirpation of all the Indians in most populous parts of the Union" by means "more destructive to the Indian natives than the conduct of the conquerors of Mexico and Peru," which would have been no small achievement. In his later years, President John Quincy Adams recognized the fate of "that hapless race of native Americans, which we are exterminating with such merciless and perfidious cruelty, [to be] among the heinous sins of this nation, for which I believe God will one day bring [it] to judgement."

Contemporary commentators see the matter differently. The prominent Cold War historian John Lewis Gaddis hails Adams as the grand strategist who laid the foundations for the Bush Doctrine that "expansion is the path to security." Plausibly, and with evident appreciation, Gaddis takes the doctrine to be routinely applicable throughout the history of the "infant empire," as George Washington termed the new Republic. Gaddis passes in silence over Adams's gory contributions to the "heinous sins of this nation" as he established the doctrine, along with the doctrine of executive war in violation of the Constitution, in a famous state paper justifying the conquest of Florida on utterly fraudulent pretexts of self-defense. The conquest was part of Adams's project of "removing or eliminating native Americans from the southeast," in the words of William Earl Weeks, the leading historian of the massacre, who provides a lurid account of the "exhibition of murder and plunder" targeting Indians and runaway slaves.

To mention another example, in the June 11, 2009, issue of one of the world's leading liberal intellectual journals, *The New York Review of Books*, political analyst Russell Baker records what he learned from the work of the "heroic historian" Edmund Morgan: namely, that Columbus and the early explorers "found a continental vastness sparsely populated by farming and hunting people. . . . In the limitless and unspoiled world stretching from tropical jungle to the frozen north, there may have been scarcely more than a million inhabitants." The calculation is off by many tens of millions, and the "vastness" included advanced civilizations, but no matter. The exercise of "genocide denial with a vengeance" merits little notice, presumably because it is so unremarkable and in a good cause.[1]

Imperial conquest illustrates another thesis that Herman and Peterson explore: what Obama's UN Ambassador Susan Rice calls the "emerging international norm that recognizes the 'responsibility to protect' innocent civilians facing death on a mass scale." It is worth bearing in mind that the norm is not "emerging," but rather venerable, and has consistently been a guiding imperial doctrine, invoked to justify the resort to violence when other pretexts are lacking.

The Spanish conquistadors in the early sixteenth century were careful to instruct the natives that if you "acknowledge the Church as the Ruler and Superior of the whole world," then we "shall receive you in all love and charity, and shall leave you, your wives, and your children, and your lands, free without servitude," and even "award you many privileges and exemptions and will grant you many benefits," fulfilling our responsibility to protect, in current terminology. But those who are protected also have responsibilities, the Spanish humanitarians sternly advised: "if you do not [meet your obligations in this way, then] we shall powerfully enter into your country, and shall make war against you in all ways and manners that we can . . . and we protest that the deaths and losses which shall accrue from this are your fault, and not that of their Highnesses, or ours, nor of these cavaliers who come with us"—words paraphrased by some Islamic extremist groups in their warnings to Western infidels, doubtless also regarding them as forthcoming and humane.

The *Requerimiento* of the Spanish conquerors had a counterpart a century later among the English colonists settling North America. To this day, the United States is reverentially admired,

at home at least, as "a city on a hill" or, as Ronald Reagan preferred, "a shining city on a hill." In April 2009, British historian
Geoffrey Hodgson was admonished by liberal *New York Times*
columnist Roger Cohen for describing the United States as "just
one great, but imperfect, country among others." Hodgson's
error, Cohen explained, is his failure to realize that unlike other
states, "America was born as an idea," as a "city on a hill," an
"inspirational notion" that resides "deep in the American psyche."
Its crimes are merely unfortunate lapses that do not tarnish the
essential nobility of America's "transcendent purpose," to borrow
the phrase of the eminent scholar Hans Morgenthau, one of the
founders of the hard-headed realist school of international relations theory, writing on "the purpose of America."

Like the Spanish, the English colonists were guided by Rice's
"emerging humanitarian norm." The inspirational phrase "city on a
hill" was coined by John Winthrop in 1630, outlining the glorious
future of a new nation "ordained by God." A year earlier, his
Massachusetts Bay Colony received its charter from the King of
England and established its Great Seal. The seal depicts an Indian
holding a spear pointing downward in a sign of peace, and pleading
with the colonists to "[c]ome over and help us." The charter states
that conversion of the population—rescuing them from their bitter
pagan fate—was "the principal end of this plantation." The English
colonists too were on a humane mission as they extirpated and
exterminated the natives—for their own good, their successors
explained. During his second term as president a century ago,
Theodore Roosevelt explained to a group of white missionaries
that "[t]he expansion of the peoples of white, or European, blood
during the past four centuries . . . has been fraught with lasting benefit to most of the peoples already dwelling in the lands over which
the expansion took place," despite what Africans, native Americans,
Filipinos, and other beneficiaries might mistakenly believe.

The vulgar politicization of the concept of genocide, and the
"emerging international norm" of humanitarian intervention,

appear to be products of the fading of the Cold War, which removed the standard pretexts for intervention while leaving intact the institutional and ideological framework for its regular practice during those years. It is not surprising, then, that in the post–Cold War era, as Herman and Peterson observe, "just as the guardians of 'international justice' have yet to find a single crime committed by a great white northern power against people of color that crosses their threshold of gravity, so too all of the fine talk about the 'responsibility to protect' and the 'end of impunity' has never once been extended to the victims of these same powers, no matter how egregious the crimes."

That outcome was forecast sixty years ago in one of the earliest decisions of the World Court, which ruled unanimously in 1949, in the Corfu Channel case, that "[t]he Court can only regard the alleged right of intervention as the manifestation of a policy of force, such as has, in the past, given rise to most serious abuses and such as cannot, whatever be the defects in international organization, find a place in international law . . . ; from the nature of things, [intervention] would be reserved for the most powerful states, and might easily lead to perverting the administration of justice itself." Intervention is like the Mississippi River, international law specialist Richard Falk once observed: it flows from north to south.

Much the same conclusion was drawn in 2004 by a high-level panel convened by the United Nations to consider the newly fashionable concept of "responsibility to protect," invoked by the United States and its allies to justify military intervention without Security Council authorization. The panel rejected this thesis, adopting the view of the South Summit—representing the traditional victims—which had condemned "the so-called 'right' of humanitarian intervention" in the wake of the NATO bombing of Serbia. The UN panel reiterated the conditions of the UN Charter that force can be deployed only when authorized by the Security Council, or under Article 51, in defense against armed attack until the Security Council acts. Article 51 is generally interpreted to allow the use of force when "the necessity for action is instant, overwhelming, and leaving no choice of means, and no moment of deliberation," in Daniel Webster's classic phrase. The panel concluded that "Article 51 needs neither extension nor restriction of its long-understood scope, . . . it should be neither rewritten nor reinterpreted." The panel added that "[f]or those impatient with such a response, the answer must be that, in a world full of perceived potential threats, the risk to the global order and the norm of nonintervention on which it continues to be based is simply too great for the legality of unilateral preventive action, as distinct from collectively endorsed action, to be accepted. Allowing one to so act is to allow all."

Allowing all to have the rights of Western powers would evidently be unthinkable. Thus when Vice President Joe Biden says (July 6, 2009) that Israel has the "sovereign right" to attack Iran, and that the United States cannot hinder any such action (with U.S. equipment) because Washington "cannot dictate to another sovereign nation what they can and cannot do," he does not mean to imply that Iran has the "sovereign right" to attack Israel if it takes seriously the regular threats of aggression by the reigning nuclear power of the region, while the United States stands by quietly. It is always necessary to recognize the maxim of Thucydides: "Right, as the world goes, is only in question between equals in power, while the strong do what they can and the weak suffer what they must." This is the fundamental operative principle of international order.

The traditional imperial powers are alone in adopting Rice's "emerging international norm" in the conventional form that she doubtless has in mind. Again, that should hardly come as much of a surprise. As for the term "genocide," perhaps the most honorable course would be to expunge it from the vocabulary until the day, if it ever comes, when honesty and integrity can become an "emerging norm."

Introduction

A remarkable degree of continuity stretches across the many decades of bribes and threats, economic sanctions, subversion, terrorism, aggression, and occupation ordered-up by the policy-making elite of the United States. But no less impressive is the continuity that can be observed in the ways these policies are understood by this elite, and by the establishment intellectuals and news media that report about them daily and reflect on or ignore their consequences.

With both its major rivals and allies in Europe and Asia devastated during the Second World War, the United States, suffering no direct damage at all, emerged from the war with a uniquely dominant economic, political, and military position in world affairs—"50% of the world's wealth but only 6.3% of its population," in the words of the famous postwar balance sheet drafted by George Kennan in early 1948 on behalf of the State Department's Policy Planning Staff.[2] U.S. leaders recognized exactly what this unprecedented advantage meant, and set out to design policies that would "permit [the United States] to maintain this position of disparity," aggressively pursuing U.S. advantages by all available means. The U.S. "military-industrial complex" mentioned by Eisenhower in January 1961, now well into its seventh decade and accounting for roughly one out of every two dollars spent on military-related purposes worldwide, and the U.S. "empire of bases" that encircles much of the globe, including the moveable bases its aircraft carrier task forces provide and the nuclear and conventional force capabilities of the ever-expanding NATO bloc, reflect and support this effort to deepen and expand the advantages attained by the United States during the war.[3]

To maintain the global structure of inequality, and in the process serve the interests of its transnational corporations anxious to enlarge their business abroad, the United States had to confront numerous nationalist upheavals by peoples in former colonial areas who sought independence, self-determination, and better lives. In the pursuit of this counterrevolutionary end, the United States regularly aligned with local military and ex-colonial comprador elites to contain and, wherever possible, to resist and roll back the kind of threat referred to by one National Security Council assessment as "an increasing popular demand for immediate improvement in the low living standards of the masses."[4] This end and this perception of "threat" accounts for the U.S. support of a string of dictatorships in Thailand, South Vietnam, Indonesia, the Philippines, South Africa, and Nigeria, to name a few, and a large number of semi-fascist "national security states" in Latin America. As has long been observed, while these states were torture-prone and deeply anti-democratic, they improved the "climate of investment" by keeping their majorities fearful, atomized, and without political recourse.[5] If local dictators failed, direct U.S. military intervention frequently followed—and, as in the cases of Vietnam and more recently Afghanistan and Iraq, sometimes with monumentally destructive human and material consequences. By one estimate, the United States carried out "extremely serious" military interventions in at least twenty-nine different countries from 1945 to 2009.[6]

Of course, the publicly expressed rationale for this regressive, no-holds-barred foreign policy was never stated to be improving the climate for investment, much less to silence indigenous demands for higher standards of living for the Third World's masses—though the opening-up of markets abroad was an objective that also fit ideological principles. Instead, the prevailing rhetoric of officials, establishment intellectuals, and the media was always "national security" and the closely linked "Soviet threat" of the Cold War system of propaganda, against which peoples, countries, and whole continents needed the kind of special protection that only the United States could provide.[7] This "threat to our whole security in the form of the men in the Kremlin" (Kennan) was regularly invoked even where ludicrously inapplicable, as in the case of the overthrow of the democratic governments of Mohammad Mosaddeq by a CIA coup in Iran in 1953 and of Jacobo Arbenz in Guatemala by a U.S.-organized mercenary invasion in 1954. But this alleged "threat" was helpful in these and many other cases, and very much an institutionalized reflex of the postwar era until the start of the 1990s; it added to the routine demonization of any U.S. target and the widespread belief in this country of its "exceptionalism," its moral superiority, and its proper immunity from international law. The result was the normalization of anything the U.S. government chose to do in the realm of foreign policy, regardless of its brutality and ˙criminality. Hence, also, the near-limitless capacity of the media and intellectual elite as well as the general public to swallow U.S.-directed or supported terrorism, aggression, crimes against humanity, and even genocide straight to the present day.

Back in the early 1970s, Noam Chomsky and one of the present authors (Herman) wrote a short study of mass killings, centering on the monumental mass killing that the United States was still carrying out in Vietnam: *Counter-Revolutionary Violence: Bloodbaths in Fact and Propaganda* (*CRV*).[8] Beyond the bloodbaths perpetrated by the United States in Vietnam (1954–1973), the other theaters of mass atrocity that they surveyed were the Philippines (1898–1973),

Thailand (1946–1973), Indonesia (1965–1969), Cambodia (1965–1973), East Pakistan (1971), and Burundi (1972). The authors took it as an obvious and readily demonstrable truth that the United States, "as a result of its dominant position and wide-ranging counter-revolutionary efforts, [had] been the most important single instigator, administrator and moral and material sustainer of serious bloodbaths in the years that followed the Second World War."[9] They also took it as obvious and demonstrable that U.S. officials, with the help of the media and establishment intellectuals, would engage in "atrocities management," producing a stream of propaganda to divert attention away from U.S.-organized and -approved violence, and onto that of its enemies. Thus there would be good and bad bloodbaths—those that should be ignored and those that should be focused-on with indignation.

Accordingly, *CRV* used as its framework of analysis four categories of bloodbaths: "Constructive," "Benign," "Nefarious," and "Mythical" (a sub-category under Nefarious). Those bloodbaths carried out by the United States itself or that serve immediate and major U.S. interests are Constructive; those carried out by allies or clients are Benign; and those carried out by U.S. target states are Nefarious and (sometimes) Mythical. Obviously, the use of these terms was partly ironic and partly serious. Nevertheless, *CRV* meant to capture something essential but otherwise unstated about the *politics of bloodbaths* and the infamy that attaches to only some of them: How bloodbaths are evaluated by the U.S. political establishment and its media, depending on who is responsible for carrying them out.

For that establishment, including the media, the U.S. invasion of Vietnam was never described as "aggression," nor was it ever described or denounced as involving a gigantic massacre, or series of massacres, or a bloodbath, or genocide, despite the killing of possibly three million or more people, with a bombing and chemical warfare program that also left very large numbers crippled and genetically damaged, along with a ravaged land. The only time a "bloodbath" threat was invoked was in considering what might happen to collaborators of the U.S. occupation forces, in the case of an eventual U.S. withdrawal. (These days, similar warnings are frequently invoked to counter any suggestion of possible U.S. withdrawals from Afghanistan or Iraq. Only we and our spunky allies in Kabul and Baghdad stand between millions of innocent lives and the Islamo-fascists of the Taliban and al Qaeda.) Vietnamese resistance killings were harshly and indignantly denounced as "terrorism" and more. The media role in protecting the real bloodbath, including their swallowing the MIA-POW gambit,[10] was all that a propaganda system could ask. And the response of the "international community" to these massive killings was extremely muted.

One small indication of the Vietnam War era media treatment of the subject is that a little 1973 book on bloodbaths was actually never published. Officials of the parent corporation, the major media firm Warner Publishing, saw the book just prior to publication, greatly disliked it, and caused it to be suppressed (and the publishing subsidiary Warner Modular was soon dissolved). The contents saw life, however, when the authors published a much-expanded version in 1979 under the title *The Washington Connection and Third World Fascism*.[11]

The framework used in those earlier works is eerily applicable to the present. The leading mainstream experts on "genocide" and mass-atrocity crimes today still carefully exclude from consideration the U.S. attacks on Indochina, as well as the 1965–1966 Indonesian massacres within that country—just as they exclude the deaths and destruction that have followed from the United States' and NATO-bloc's aggressive wars of the past decade.

The recipient of the 2003 Pulitzer Prize in the General Nonfiction category, Samantha Power's *"A Problem from Hell": America and the Age of Genocide*, devotes only one sentence to Indonesia, ignoring entirely the mass killings of 1965–1966, mentioning only its invasion-occupation of East Timor in 1975 and after. Power writes that Indonesia killed "between 100,000 and 200,000 civilians" in East Timor; she then adds, falsely, that the "United States looked away," when in fact the United States and its British and Australian allies supplied both the weapons and diplomatic cover for Indonesia's bloody campaign without interruption for nearly a quarter-century (1975–1999). Power's cursory treatment of the U.S. wars in Vietnam and Cambodia and the massive U.S. killings in both countries turns up only in the chapter devoted to life in Cambodia under the Khmer Rouge, where she notes in passing that "U.S. B-52 raids killed tens of thousands of civilians" and "indirectly helped give rise to a monstrous regime."[12] Notice that in Power's hands, the "monstrous regime" is the one that arose after the other regime's bombers "killed tens of thousands of civilians"—but no negative adjectives are applied to the regime that sent along those bombers from the other side of the planet.

Roy Gutman and David Rieff's *Crimes of War* has no entry for Vietnam or Indonesia; and under none of this encyclopedia-like volume's seven entries for Act of War, Aggression, Crimes against Peace, Crimes against Humanity, Genocide, Systematic Rape, and War Crimes is there a single example drawn from the U.S. war against Vietnam or Indonesia's war against its peasant population. Instead, under the entry for Cambodia, Sydney Schanberg, the former *New York Times* reporter and protagonist in the Hollywood film *The Killing Fields*, informs readers of the "great irony" resulting from the 1970 U.S. overthrow of Cambodia's Prince Sihanouk and the years of massive bombings and eventual U.S. ground invasion—not the death and destruction they entailed, but only the rise of the Khmer Rouge, a "motley collection of ineffectual guerrilla bands totaling at most three thousand to five thousand men" when the United States started to bomb Cambodia in the 1960s, but transformed "into the murderous force of seventy thousand to 100,000 that swept into Phnom Penh five years later...."[13]

Similarly, Aryeh Neier's book *War Crimes* says little about the U.S. aggression against Vietnam or Cambodia and nothing about Indonesia's killing fields—Neier treats Vietnam simply as the stage upon which the My Lai massacre of 1968 was eventually played out.[14] International law barrister and former appellate judge with the UN Special Court for Sierra Leone Geoffrey Robertson's assessment of the "Thirty Inglorious Years" that followed the adoption of the Universal Declaration of Human Rights (1948), the Genocide Convention (1948), and the four Geneva Conventions (1949) refers to the twenty-year Vietnam War as nothing more than "America's lamentable mistake [*sic*[15]] to shore up the vicious Catholic dictator, Ngo Dinh Diem"— though like Neier, Robertson mentions that a "few firefight atrocities" such as My Lai "were brought to account."[16]

Vietnam and Indonesia were also ignored by CNN chief foreign correspondent Christiane Amanpour in her late 2008 documentary *Scream Bloody Murder*, an examination of "genocide around the world." But Amanpour's "world" was limited to politically acceptable cases, Nefarious genocides—Germany under the Nazis, Cambodia under the Khmer Rouge, Iraq under Saddam Hussein, Bosnia and Herzegovina from 1992 to 1995, Rwanda in 1994, and Darfur this decade.[17] Vietnam and Indonesia were also never mentioned as cases in point in the December 2008 report by the U.S.-based Genocide Prevention Task Force, *Preventing Genocide*.[18]

In short, the vast killing fields of Vietnam and Indonesia, which belonged to the category of Constructive bloodbaths in 1973, remain firmly in that category today; and the other bloodbath categories apply now with the same political bias and rigor, as we describe below. As the U.S. government and its proxy regimes in Saigon and Jakarta were the perpetrators of these mass-atrocity crimes, the victims were rarely acknowledged, the crimes against them rarely punished (with only low-level personnel brought to book in well-publicized cases like My Lai), and the most serious crimes of all—the U.S. aggressions against Vietnam, Cambodia, and Laos, the U.S. genocide against the south of Vietnam, and the Indonesian genocides against Indonesians in 1965–1966, and the East Timorese from 1975 on—remain outside the ambit of Western humanitarian concern and the reach of Western-enforced "international justice."

This highly politicized usage even has a humorous tinge—as we now supposedly live in an age of high sensitivity to human rights abuses, when a "responsibility to protect" (R2P) civilian populations against acts of "genocide, war crimes, crimes against humanity, and ethnic cleansing" has been proclaimed by the unanimous assent of the UN General Assembly[19] and when the International Criminal Court (ICC) has been empowered to "put an end to impunity for the perpetrators" of "atrocities that deeply shock the conscience of humanity," in the words of the Preamble to the Rome Statute that created the Court.[20]

In an amazing "end of impunity" set of coincidences, it turns out that all fourteen of the ICC's indictments through mid-2009 had been issued against black Africans from three countries (the Democratic Republic of Congo, Uganda, and the Sudan[21]), while carefully excluding Uganda's Yoweri Museveni and Rwanda's Paul Kagame, perhaps the most prolific tandem of killers to rule on the African continent during the current era, but highly valued clients of the West. Indeed, Kagame especially is an adored figure throughout much of the West, feted as a great liberator and statesman on his many visits to North America, while at home "he plays host to visiting members of the global—and particularly the American—power elite," in the words of the liberal *New Yorker* magazine, his guests including Bill Clinton, Pastor Rick Warren, Google's CEO Eric Schmidt, and Harvard Business School's Michael Porter, "all friends of Kagame and members of his kitchen cabinet of advisers."[22] Kagame also appeared as a guest on Amanpour's *Scream Bloody Murder* program, where he was treated graciously.

It is also notable that the ICC's statute, like the rules governing the International Criminal Tribunal for the Former Yugoslavia (ICTY) as well as the International Criminal Tribunal for Rwanda (ICTR), excludes from its jurisdiction the crime of aggression. At Nuremberg, however, this was judged to be "not only an international crime" but the *supreme international crime* differing only from other war crimes in that it contains within itself the accumulated evil of the whole."[23] Human rights groups such as Amnesty International and Human Rights Watch (HRW) also exclude aggression as a proper area for their inquiries. Defending what it called its official policy of "neutrality" on questions of war and peace as the United States and the United Kingdom prepared to launch their March 2003 aggression against Iraq, HRW explained that it "does not make judgments about the decision whether to go to war" and "does not support or oppose the threatened war with Iraq. We do not opine on whether the dangers to civilians in Iraq and neighboring countries of launching a war are greater or lesser than the dangers to U.S. or allied civilians—or, ultimately, the Iraqi people—of not launching one. We make no comment on the intense debate surrounding the legality of President George Bush's proposed doctrine of 'pre-emptive self-defense' or the need for U.N. Security Council approval of a war."[24]

Surely this pretense of "neutrality" results because the United States wants itself and its principal client to be free to commit the supreme international crime and therefore the mass-atrocity crimes that follow from it, which they have done often and for many years, and with complete impunity. The adaptation of "international justice" to this principle of exclusion—along with its acceptance by establishment media and intellectuals—tells us clearly that the system is nicely adjusted to the needs of the powerful.

Both in its statute and its practices, the ICC has been no better than the *ad hoc* tribunals for Yugoslavia and Rwanda. Like them, the ICC practices selective investigation, selective prosecution—and, on the other side of the aisle, selective impunity.

The history of great power crimes against the peace, crimes against humanity, war crimes, ethnic cleansing, and genocide shows the centrality of racism to the imperial project. The powerful, the people at the center of this project, have always tended to be white European or North American, their victims darker. The conquest of the Western Hemisphere and the wiping-out of its indigenous peoples were carried out over many decades, with very modest opposition from within the morally enlightened Christian world. The African slave trade resulted in millions of deaths in the initial capture and transatlantic crossing, with a cruel degradation for the survivors. The steady massacres and subjugation of black Africans within Africa itself rested on "an unquestioning belief in the innate superiority of the white race, . . . the very bedrock of imperial attitudes," essential to making the business of mass slaughter "morally acceptable," John Ellis writes. "At best, the Europeans regarded those they slaughtered with little more than amused contempt."[25] This dynamic has always been accompanied by a process of projection, whereby the victims of slaughter and dispossession are depicted as "merciless Indian savages" (the Declaration of Independence) by the racist savages whose superior weapons, greed, and ruthlessness gave them the ability to conquer, destroy, and exterminate.

The dominant institutions today may be more complex than five hundred or five thousand years ago, but, at bottom, they work no differently than have their predecessors throughout the ages. Great aggressors project their ugliest traits onto their victims (the "terrorists," the "militants," and the religious "fascists" and "ethnic cleansers" of the twenty-four-hour news day), even as they kill halfway around the world in the name of the Homeland. Demonization of the real victims and atrocities management remain as important as ever and keep the citizens of the imperial powers properly misinformed and supportive of big-time atrocities. The path from the "White Man's Burden" to the regimes of selective "human rights" and "international justice" has been a lot more direct than its current-day travelers like to believe. Western "liberals" follow the same flags as do their right-wing counterparts;[26] and when handed the same bloody portfolio but with a new label that reads "Change We Can Believe In," often outgun them as well.[27]

Thus President Barack Obama's UN Ambassador, Susan E. Rice, has long been an "advocate of 'dramatic action' against genocide" and "mass killings," the New York Times reported. Like so many of her contemporaries, Rice believes there is an "emerging international norm that recognizes the 'responsibility to protect' innocent civilians facing death on a mass scale and whose governments cannot or will not protect them"—and "Never," she adds, "is the international responsibility to protect more compelling than in cases of genocide." But as with the rest of the U.S. policy-making elite, it is uncontested for Rice that this alleged norm works in one direction only: From Washington toward the rest of the world, with the United States the chief lawmaker, enforcer, judge, and jury. "[T]he international community has a responsibility to protect civilian populations from violations of international humanitarian law when states are unwilling or unable to do so," Rice told the Security Council in her inaugural address in late January 2009. Singling out "5 million deaths" in the Democratic Republic of Congo (DRC), the rebel Lord's Resistance Army in Uganda which "has for many years terrorized civilian populations," and the "genocide in Darfur," Rice went on to say that the "United States is steadfast in its commitment to safeguard human rights and end violations of international humanitarian law, both in conjunction with the United Nations, and through our other efforts throughout the world."[28]

Notice that Rice's catalogue of R2P-worthy populations in Central Africa made no mention of the prolific body counts that the U.S. clients Museveni and Kagame have left in their wakes, and who since 1996 have largely carved up the DRC between them, helping to cause a death toll more than fifteen times the

scale of the "genocide in Darfur." (See "Rwanda and the Democratic Republic of Congo," below. Also our "Concluding Note.") Nor, needless to say, did Rice show the slightest recognition of her own government's commitment to violating international humanitarian law and the UN Charter, and the mass killings at which it excels—the international community's alleged "responsibility to protect civilian populations" simply does not extend to the victims of the government in which Rice serves.

Consider how Iraq, one of the major theaters of mass-atrocity crimes over the last three decades, is made to fit into the current R2P doctrine. Expressing a view that is standard among the R2P advocates, the International Coalition for the Responsibility to Protect maintains that the U.S.–U.K. invasion of Iraq could not have been justified on "humanitarian" grounds. Although "gross human rights violations occurred in Iraq in the 1980s and 1990s, these crimes were not occurring, nor likely to happen, at the time of the 2003 military intervention." For this reason, the invasion "failed to meet the [guiding R2P] criteria legitimizing the use of military intervention."29

We find this argument remarkable, both for what it takes into consideration and what it leaves out. Notice that in the judgment of this Coalition, the relevant question is whether the government of Iraq had been committing "gross human rights violations . . . at the time of the 2003 military intervention." Left unasked is whether the United States and Britain had been responsible for gross human rights violations during the years they enforced the "sanctions of mass destruction" (1990–2003), whether they were on the verge of committing even more egregious human rights violations by invading Iraq (*ca.* 2002–early 2003), and whether they did in fact commit gross human rights violations from March 19–20, 2003, on, including a death toll that may top one million Iraqis, with millions more driven from their homes. (See "The Iraq Invasion-Occupation," below.) Thus in this global acid-test for R2P in the first decade of the 21st century, these R2P advocates can freely debate the need for the U.S.–U.K. invasion to protect Iraq's population against the Iraqi regime. But neither these nor any other R2P advocate can even raise the question of the need for a military intervention to protect Iraq's population against the U.S.–U.K. invaders. The United States and its allies simply could not kill a sufficiently large number of foreign nationals for R2P and ICC enthusiasts and spokespersons to suggest that R2P and the ICC be invoked to stop them.

What this means is that advocacy on behalf of victims by R2P and ICC campaigners and spokespersons depends on whom their tormentors are: If victims of the government of the Sudan, the Lord's Resistance Army in Uganda, or certain nongovernmental armed groups operating in the Democratic Republic of Congo and the Central African Republic, then *yes*, they are worthy of attention, their suffering matters, and the U.S. ambassador is ready to denounce their tormentors before the world; but if victims of the Ugandan People's Defense Forces or the Rwandan Patriotic Front, then *no*, they fall within the vast cohort of victims unworthy of our attention, and merit at best a passing mention. Even more striking, what this does not mean is advocacy on behalf of victims within the Occupied Palestinian Territories, or the U.S. war zones of Afghanistan, Iraq, Pakistan, and beyond— theaters where the responsibility for mass killings falls closer to home, and where the responsibility to protect these victims would entail protecting them against Rice's own government above all.

On July 23, 2009, the Nicaraguan Catholic priest and then-President of the UN General Assembly Miguel d'Escoto Brockmann hosted the first of a three-day "Thematic Dialogue" at the United Nations devoted to the "responsibility to protect" doctrine.[30] The list of presenters invited to address the General Assembly included Noam Chomsky of the United States and Belgium's Jean Bricmont,[31] two serious critics of R2P, as well as Australia's Gareth Evans.

Perhaps no single individual has done more to raise the profile of R2P and to place it on the UN's agenda than Evans. He is the author of a 2008 book on R2P[32] serves as the co-Chair of the International Advisory Board of the Global Center for the Responsibility to Protect at City University of New York, was co-Chair of the International Commission on Intervention and State Sovereignty, which produced the 2001 report *The Responsibility to Protect* [33] that helped bring this phrase into common usage, and is a past president of the International Crisis Group.

But before all of this, Evans served as the Foreign Minister of Australia (1988–1996). It was while performing in this role that he was instrumental to Australia's completion of the 1989 Timor Gap Oil Treaty with Indonesia that granted Australian firms the right to explore and drill in the oil-rich "Indonesian province of East Timor," in the treaty's terms. With this treaty, Evans placed Australia squarely in that rare camp of states that recognized Indonesia's illegal conquest of East Timorese territory by force in 1975—despite some 200,000 deaths in East Timor as a "result of the Indonesian invasion and occupation," roughly a "third of the population, or proportionately more than were killed in Cambodia under Pol Pot."[34]

At a news conference following their presentations before the General Assembly, a UN reporter asked Gareth Evans to explain the "guidelines" that R2P advocates will observe before they recommend military intervention, the ultimate stage of R2P action. "How can you possibly come to an agreement on the language to use so that you can apply [R2P] without it still being abused?" the reporter wondered. "How do you define the worst possible crimes?"

The R2P doctrine "defines itself," Evans replied, "in the sense that genocide, war crimes, crimes against humanity, and ethnic cleansing are all inherently conscience-shocking, and by their very nature of a scale that demands a response, whether preventive or reactive. . . ."

"It's really impossible to be precise about numbers here," Evans continued. "In some cases you're fearing scores-of-thousands, hundreds-of-thousands, or even millions of casualties. . . ." But, he added, "In other cases the numbers are much smaller. We remember *starkly* the horror of Srebrenica and there you're talking about seven or eight thousand people as compared with numbers in the millions. Was Račak with its forty-five victims in Kosovo in '99 sufficient to trigger the response that was triggered by the international community?"

"The short point is don't misplay the numbers game, calibrating the extent of one's outrage by reference to whether it's X or Y numbers," Evans concluded. "I take the view that once you cross a certain threshold, you're in the realm of just conscience-shocking catastrophe which demands a response one way or the other. . . . There's no cookie-cutter approach, I'm afraid, you can adapt to any of this stuff."

"There *is* a way to calibrate reaction," Noam Chomsky interrupted. "If it's a crime of somebody else, particularly an enemy, then we're utterly outraged. If it's our own crime, either comparable or worse, either it's suppressed or denied. That works with almost 100 percent precision."[35]

In fact, the "cookie-cutter approach" is displayed dramatically by Gareth Evans himself, who singles out Račak and Srebrenica, assaulted by Serb armies, as situations demanding a response— but not East Timor, invaded and occupied by Indonesia, or the Gaza Strip, assaulted and starved by Israel, or whole countries such as Afghanistan and Iraq, with their vulnerable populations under attack by the United States and its allies.[36]

We find that Evans' "cookie-cutter" is the standard establishment approach, with choices regularly made that have nothing to do with crossing certain thresholds of scale, much less with whether events are inherently conscience-shocking. Instead, the distinction turns on *who* does *what* to *whom*—and *where does power lie*.

Once again, we are back to the difference between Constructive, Nefarious, Benign, and Mythical bloodbaths. Let us examine some of them by category in more detail.

Constructive Genocides

In terms of the number of human lives taken and the awareness among policymakers that this was the likely consequence of their policies, perhaps the largest genocidal action of the last thirty years was the economic sanctions imposed upon Iraq following Iraq's invasion of Kuwait in August 1990. First adopted by Security Council Resolution 661 to compel Iraq's withdrawal from Kuwait, the U.S. and British victors in the 1991 war on Iraq pressed the Council to adopt a new Resolution 687, following Iraq's defeat, that demanded the destruction of Iraq's chemical, biological, and nuclear weapons programs, as well as its ballistic missiles; a Special Commission was created to supervise Iraq's compliance.[37] In this way, a mechanism was established that enabled the United States and Britain, by denying that Iraq was in compliance with UN 687, to compel the Special Commission and Security Council to find that Iraq was not in compliance, thereby preventing the lifting of the sanctions.

Enforced chiefly by the U.S. and British governments, UN 687's devastating sanctions prevented Iraq from repairing its water, sanitation, and electrical systems, all of which were deliberately destroyed during the massive bombing attacks of the war. A postwar assessment by the *New York Times* of the "Bush Administration's internal findings" on the damage inflicted by the U.S. bombing campaign reported that "Iraq has, for some time to come, been relegated to a pre-industrial age, but with all the disabilities of post-industrial dependency on an intensive use of energy and technology." One confidential source, who "played a central role in the air campaign," even admitted to the *Washington Post* that so-called "Strategic bombing . . . strikes [were aimed] against 'all those things that allow a nation to sustain itself'"[38]—all those things "indispensable to the survival of [Iraq's] civilian population," to use the phrasing of the 1979 Protocol Additional to the Geneva Conventions.[39]

Over the next thirteen years, none of these systems was returned to their pre-war state. Thomas Nagy observes that as early as January 22, 1991, just days into the bombing phase of the war, the U.S. Defense Intelligence Agency predicted that as Iraq depends on the importation of "specialized equipment and some chemicals" to supply its people with clean water, the failure to "secure supplies will result in a shortage of pure drinking water for much of the population," and lead to "increased incidences, if not epidemics, of disease." Based on this and subsequent U.S. planning documents, Nagy concludes that the "United States knew sanctions had the capacity to devastate the water treatment system of Iraq. It knew what the consequences would be: increased outbreaks of disease and high rates of child mortality. . . . The United States has deliberately pursued a policy of destroying the water treatment system of Iraq, knowing full well the cost in Iraqi lives."[40]

The sanctions and the Sanctions Committee's power to dispense or to withhold repair projects led Denis Halliday, the first UN Coordinator for Humanitarian Affairs in Iraq, to resign his post in 1998, calling the impact of the sanctions "genocide." His successor, Hans von Sponeck, quickly reached the same conclusion and resigned as well. A UN assessment in 1999 found "continuing degradation of the Iraqi economy with an acute deterioration in the living conditions of the Iraqi population and severe strains on its social fabric. . . . [T]he Iraqi people would not be undergoing such deprivations in the absence of the prolonged measures adopted by the Security Council and the effects of war."[41]A mortality survey carried out jointly that same year by UNICEF and the World Health Organization estimated that "children under five are dying at twice the rate they were [in 1989]," and that had this not been the case, half a million more children would have been alive at the end of the decade.[42]

This phase of the great Iraqi bloodbath "was not accidental nor the result of ignorance," von Sponeck writes. "While [the U.S.–U.K. representatives on the Sanctions Committee] would painstakingly scrutinize Iraq Government orders for electricity spare parts and replacement equipment and would, phase by phase, block significant numbers of purchase requests for areas under Baghdad's jurisdiction, the Sanctions Committee approved, with rare exceptions, all orders for Kurdistan."[43] The same pattern was repeated for all infrastructure repair requests, as "almost 100 percent of all items put on hold by the sanctions committee of the UN Security Council during the oil-for-food programme period (1996–2003) was due to the U.S. and U.K. governments." The sanctions regime "indiscriminately punished the Iraqi population as a whole," von Sponeck writes elsewhere, and was judged "unequivocally illegal under existing international humanitarian law and human rights law" by the UN Economic and Social Council.[44] Indeed, this murderous economic warfare was labeled "sanctions of mass destruction" by John Mueller and Karl Mueller in 1999; they estimated that the sanctions had "been a necessary cause of the deaths of more people in Iraq than have been slain by all so-called weapons of mass destruction throughout history."[45]

The normalization of this deliberate U.S. mass killing of civilians was starkly revealed in May 1996, when CBS TV's Lesley

sion and occupation), among other cases of mass killings.[47] The table shows that there were only eighty references to "genocide" stemming from the sanctions regime, whereas for Bosnia, Kosovo, Rwanda, and Darfur, four Nefarious cases, the usage ran to 481, 323, 3,199, and 1,172, respectively, despite the much greater toll from the Iraq sanctions in all but the Rwanda case; and for the Congo, a Benign case, usage was a mere seventeen.

If we use the Iraq Economic Sanctions period as our base period for comparison, setting the eighty instances of media use of "genocide" to describe this period equal to the number 1, we see in Column 4 of Table 1 the extent of media bias. The bare ratios for usage of these six cases of mass killings are 0.2 for the 2003–2009 war ("genocide" was used to describe this period one-fifth as often as the Sanctions period), 6 for Bosnia (six times as often), 4 for Kosovo, 40 for Rwanda, 15 for Darfur, and only 0.2 for the Congo (unlike the Sanctions period and the Iraq war, this is a Benign case). Adjusting these for the actual numbers killed, the ratios of death tolls to usage of "genocide" flies out of sight for Iraq and especially for the Congo (see Column 5), where the victims are very numerous but unworthy, in contrast with the victims of Western targets. As we will see, the bias is maintained for other bloodbaths based on their political status.

2. THE IRAQ INVASION-OCCUPATION

It is notorious that the U.S. media, some by their own belated admission,[48] served as virtual government press agents during the eighteen-month run-up to the March 2003 invasion of Iraq. Although the devastating effects of the ongoing U.S. war and occupation have been harder to ignore than were the effects of the thirteen-year-long sanctions regime (largely because U.S. troops have been on the scene and suffering significant casualties, though only a small percentage of the total), the major political, media, and intellectual sectors of the U.S. establishment still have proven remarkably able to downplay the suffering and human losses of Iraq's civilian population.

When serious studies estimated Iraqi deaths since the start of the war in March 2003 at 98,000, then climbed to 655,000, and then again to more than one million, with the overwhelming majority of these deaths attributed to violent causes,[49] the media and intellectuals rarely treated Iraqi deaths as a consequence—direct or indirect—of the invasion-occupation, let alone as a deliberately imposed bloodbath, crime against humanity, or "genocide." Readers may be sure that in the context of Iraq coverage, the media never quoted Nuremberg's Judgment or alluded to the U.S. war as a "supreme international crime" and to its statement that the "accumulated evil of the whole"—hence, responsibility as well—flows from the central act of aggression.[50] Also notable is the fact that in this case where their government was the aggressor, clearly violating the UN Charter by invading another country, the establishment media and intellectuals almost uniformly ignored questions about its compatibility with the rule of law. In their study of the New York Times's coverage of the war, Howard Friel and Richard Falk found that, "despite the fact that an invasion of one country by another implicated the most fundamental aspects of the UN Charter and international law, the New York Times's editorial page never mentioned the words 'UN Charter' or 'international law' in any of its seventy editorials on Iraq from September 11, 2001, to March 21, 2003."[51] The media also failed to grant knowledgeable critics of this planned act of aggression the time and space to express their beliefs and to call for accountability for the responsible political leaders, though they have welcomed commentators eager to dismiss such concerns.

The same holds true (if to a lesser degree of exclusion) for the general humanitarian disaster in Iraq, including a displacement crisis that remains one of the world's gravest, with at one time well

TABLE 1: Differential attributions of "genocide" to different theaters
          of atrocities [A]

Col. 1	Col. 2	Col. 3	Col. 4	Col. 5
Theater: Perpetrator or Cause	Estimated Deaths per Theater	Print Media Use of 'Genocide' per Theater	Ratio of 'Genocide' Usage (80, Iraq Sanctions as Base [B]	Ratio of Deaths to 'Genocide' Usage [C]
Iraqi Population: Economic Sanctions	800,000	80	1	10,000 to 1
Iraqi Population: The U.S.–U.K. War and Occupation	1,000,000	13 [D]	0.2	76,923 to 1
Bosnian Muslims	33,000	13[D]	6	69 to 1
Kosovo Albanians	4,000	323	4	12 to 1
Rwanda	800,000	3,199	40	250 to 1
Dem. Rep. of Congo	5,400,000	17	0.2	317,647 to 1
Darfur	300,000	1,172	15	256 to 1

[A] Factiva database searches carried out under the "Newspapers: All" category in January 2009. The exact search parameters are described in note 47. We used the database operators *w/5* and * to capture all variations of the word "genocide" (e.g., genocidal, *genocidaires*) occurring anywhere in the title or text within five words of the other primary search term; and we used the limiter *not* to exclude all items that also mentioned any one or more of the other search terms.

[B] This table adopts the number 80 (Row 1, Col. 3) as its base for all subsequent calculations; the totals in Col. 4 result from the totals in Col. 3 divided by 80.

[C] The totals in Col. 5 result from the totals in Col. 2 divided by the totals in Col. 3.

[D] See Table 2, below.

over four million Iraqis having been driven from their homes, roughly half of them fleeing to neighboring countries.[52] Only modest attention was given to the destruction and looting of Iraq's archaeological heritage, perhaps the most valuable in the entire world. The assault started with the first Gulf War in 1991, but greatly escalated from March 2003 into an incalculable cultural disaster. Eleanor Robson of All Souls College, Oxford, placed its seriousness in historical perspective: "You'd have to go back centuries, to the Mongol invasion of Baghdad in 1258, to find looting on this scale."[53] The U.S. leadership keeps good company.

It should also be noted that the pre-invasion bombing campaign, launched by the U.S. and U.K. governments to destroy what remained of Iraq's air defenses as part of their preparation for the 2003 invasion, went unreported by the news media until three years later.[54] But in 2002, the tonnage of bombs dropped on Iraq by U.S. and U.K. fighter-bombers rose from zero in March, to 54.6 tons in September, and 53.2 tons in December.[55] Remarkably, although Iraq complained about these *offensive breaches of the peace*, nobody paid attention, despite the fact that Iraq filed documentation about them on a regular basis with the UN Security Council and the Secretary-General, as it had been doing for many years.[56] This actual start of this second phase of the great Iraqi bloodbath, as early as the spring of 2002, was never reported by any contemporaneous U.S. source we have been able to find.

Nor have the illegalities of U.S. policy during the occupation been carefully examined now that the removal of the former regime has been accomplished. With UN Security Council Resolution 1546 in early June 2004,[57] the United States even managed to secure retroactive legitimation of its military seizure of a sovereign country. In letters reproduced in the Annex to this breathtaking rewriting of history, Iraqi Prime Minister Ayad Allawi, who had been imposed by the Coalition Provisional Authority (i.e., by the occupying U.S. forces) only days before, requested that the U.S. military remain in Iraq as the leader of the so-called Multinational Force; in U.S. Secretary of State Colin Powell's reply, the United States solemnly pledged to do so. For its part, the Security Council played along with this farce, accepting that the "multinational force in Iraq is at the request of the incoming Interim Government. . . ," thereby adding the Council's *de jure* seal of approval to the U.S. invasion-occupation, the gravest violation of the UN Charter in recent memory. Also unexamined by the media is the Status of Forces Agreement between the Iraqi government of Prime Minister Nouri al-Maliki and the U.S. invader-occupier, which grants U.S. forces colonial privileges.[58] Also contrary to international law will be any new legislation drafted under a military occupation that governs all facets of the extraction and shipment of Iraq's oil and gas resources, as well as the distribution of the revenues. The latter is particularly contentious and was still incomplete well into 2009, as the Kurdish Regional Government remains eager to strike its own deals and serious tensions are growing inside Iraq between the Kurdish north and the Arab south.[59]

The April and later November 2004 attacks that destroyed much of Fallujah and depopulated a city of some 250,000 inhabitants have been compared to the Nazis' 1937 bombing of Guernica, Spain,[60] although these were much larger assaults than that carried out by the Nazis, with vastly more sophisticated and lethal weaponry and firepower, and left more devastation and casualties. But with civilian killings largely kept off the official books, and, even when acknowledged, treated tolerantly for these unworthy victims, such killings and bloodbaths by the United States and its allies have been thoroughly normalized. High officials of the new Obama administration display no guilt about the mass killing and devastation caused by their predecessor. Indeed, in their view, it is the Iraqis who owe the United States a debt. As Vice President Joseph Biden explained, "We've expended our blood and treasure in order to back their commitment to their constitution"[61]—a bald-faced lie, as the U.S. "investment" was

TABLE 2: Attributions of "genocide" in the case of Iraq, 2004–2008 [A]

Perpetrator–Cause of the Genocide	Print Media Use of 'Genocide'
The 2003 War and Occupation	13
The 13-Year Sanctions Regime	3
The Saddam Hussein Regime	48
Sectarian Conflict or Post-U.S. Withdrawal	54
Other–Irrelevant	30

[A]   Factiva database searches carried out under the "Newspapers: All" category in January 2009. The exact search parameters were those used in Table 1, Row 2. (See note 62.)

based on the fabricated threat of Iraq's "weapons of mass destruction" and on the real aim of projecting U.S. power into this oil-rich region. Biden's statement also ignores the monumentally greater costs in Iraqi blood and treasure exacted by his government's "supreme international crime."

Amusingly, we can see in Table 2 that while thirteen newspaper references to "genocide" in Iraq in the years 2004–2008 deal with the effects of the invasion-occupation, more than triple that number, forty-eight, apply the word to Saddam Hussein's long-since defunct regime, and fifty-four mention it to describe the possible consequences of a civil war or a U.S. withdrawal.[62] As in the case of Vietnam, the real bloodbath, engineered by the United States, cannot be acknowledged; only enemies and targets of the United States can commit the crime officially labeled "genocide."

Nefarious Genocides

1. THE DARFUR WARS AND KILLINGS

Samantha Power once marveled about how the government in Khartoum "could hardly have predicted that an obscure, inaccessible Muslim region like Darfur would become a *cause célèbre* in America."[63] Power is naive, ignoring the obvious facts that have made Darfur a predictably well-qualified candidate for a focus on villainy: That its government is dominated by Muslim Arabs; that the Sudan possesses oil, but that it is China rather than the United States or the West which has developed a strong relationship with Khartoum; and that the United States and Israel need distractions from their own human rights atrocities and those of their allies plundering the neighboring Democratic Republic of Congo.

Thus we read in Table 1 that "genocide" was used to describe Khartoum's conduct in Darfur (i.e., inside the Sudan) ninety times as frequently as it was used to describe U.S. conduct in Iraq, a foreign country seized via a war of aggression and where more than three times as many people died during the same years (2003–2009).

In fact, this far lower death toll in Darfur had already begun to receive full "genocide" billing within twelve months of the Sudan

Liberation Movement/Army's first armed attacks on Sudanese military posts and its accompanying political declaration in February and March 2003.[64] By March 2004, perhaps ten thousand people had died in Darfur and upwards of one million had fled their homes. Lobbying for foreign intervention, Mukesh Kapila, the UN Humanitarian Coordinator for the Sudan, called this the "world's greatest humanitarian and human rights catastrophe" and "possibly the world's hottest war." The only question in Kapila's mind was whether the events should be designated "ethnic cleansing" or "genocide."[65]

Rhetoric such as this is crafted to elicit action: In the face of mass-atrocity crimes, we must do something—and even doing nothing is a form of doing something, as one of the tenets of "humanitarian" and R2P-type interventionism would have us believe. Calling Darfur an "Unnoticed Genocide," the American Eric Reeves wrote in the *Washington Post*: "[P]eople are being destroyed because of who they are, racially and ethnically—'as such,' to cite the key phrase from the 1948 U.N. Convention on Genocide."[66] Unveiling his Action Plan to Prevent Genocide, Secretary-General Kofi Annan singled out Darfur of all the world's conflicts "with a deep sense of foreboding," likening it to the situation in Rwanda ten years earlier and adding that "Whatever terms it uses to describe the situation, the international community cannot stand idle."[67]

As Mahmood Mamdani puts it, such rhetoric is also a "reduction of a complex political context to a morality tale unfolding in a world populated by villains and victims who never trade places and so can always and easily be told apart." In this "simple moral world," where "evil confronts good" and "atrocities mount geometrically," a group of "perpetrators clearly identifiable as 'Arabs' confront victims clearly identifiable as 'Africans'"—and the "victim [is] untainted and the perpetrator [is] simply evil."[68] Typical of this comic-book genre is the work of *New York Times* columnist Nicholas Kristof, who "from the outset," Mamdani adds, portrayed Darfur as a "contest between 'Sudan's Arab rulers' and 'black African Sudanese'." "The killings are being orchestrated by the Arab-dominated Sudanese government, partly through the Janjaweed militia, made up of Arab raiders armed by the government," Kristof wrote in March 2004, emphasizing the almost other worldliness of the Arab government in Khartoum. "The victims are non-Arabs: blacks in the Zaghawa, Massaliet and Fur tribes. 'The Arabs want to get rid of anyone with black skin', Youssef Yakob Abdullah said. In the area of Darfur that he fled, 'there are no blacks left'."[69]

But the distinction made by Kristof, Power, Reeves, and their many allies in the Save Darfur campaign between Sudan's Arab rulers and their black African victims falsely racializes the conflict. As the 2005 Report of the International Commission of Inquiry on Darfur concluded, any rendering of the conflicts in the western Sudan as "African" versus "Arab" mistakes *political* identities, which are the consequences of these conflicts, as their causes. "The various tribes that have been the object of attacks and killings (chiefly the Fur, Masalit and Zaghawa tribes) do not appear to make up ethnic groups distinct from the ethnic group to which persons or militias that attack them belong," the Commission stated. "They speak the same language (Arabic) and embrace the same religion (Islam)."[70] Contrary to Kristof *et al.*, the government in Khartoum is comprised of black Africans no different than the black Africans in the western Sudan that oppose it. The relevant distinction in the Western Sudan is thus a political one that turns on *supporting* the government ("Arab") versus *opposing* it ("African"). The alleged "Arab-African divide" is one that has been "fanned by the growing insistence on such a divide in some circles and in the media" (in particular the white European and U.S. media); it is a process that has "contributed to the consolidation of the contrast and gradually created a marked polarisation in the perception and self-perception of the groups concerned."[71] The "Crisis in Darfur" is thus a kind of blank slate upon which Western moralists have projected foreign categories that betray the nature of the interest *they* take in the conflict, but do not reflect the realities or genuine needs of the people involved.

Additionally, the UN Environment Program argued in an extensive 2007 survey that the "underlying causes" of the conflicts in Darfur were to be found in factors such as regional climate instability, drought, desertification, population growth, food insecurity, and over-exploitation of scarce resources; it concluded that "Darfur is degraded to the extent that it cannot sustainably support its rural population." Referring to this report, Secretary-General Ban Ki-moon noted that "Almost invariably, we discuss Darfur in a convenient military and political shorthand—an ethnic conflict pitting Arab militias against black rebels and farmers. Look to its roots, though, and you discover a more complex dynamic. Amid the diverse social and political causes, the Darfur conflict began as an ecological crisis, arising at least in part from climate change. . . . It is no accident that the violence in Darfur erupted during the drought." Another report issued in 2007 by a "blue-ribbon panel of retired admirals and generals" for the CNA Corporation noted similarly that "Struggles that appear to be tribal, sectarian, or nationalist in nature are often triggered by reduced water supplies or reductions in agricultural productivity." This report added that the "situation in Darfur . . . had land resources at its root. . . . Probably more than any other recent conflict, Darfur provides a case study of how existing marginal situations can be exacerbated beyond the tipping point by climate-related factors."[72]

Still, the publicity generated over the course of 2004 by the framing of Darfur as the "unnoticed genocide" without doubt ranks as the most successful propaganda campaign of its kind this decade. Always alleged to be spiraling out of control, despite the fact that, through the end of 2008, Darfur benefited from the "largest humanitarian aid operation in the world, with more than

80 organizations and 15,000 aid workers," and had received this kind of high-priority response for five consecutive years;[73] and yet always labeled "forgotten" or "ignored," despite the fact that even when it was alleged to be at its most ignored, Darfur already had become the most heavily publicized crisis in the world.[74]

"It is time to move against the regime officials who are responsible for the killing," the International Crisis Group's John Prendergast urged in July 2004. "The sands of the Sahara should not be allowed to swallow the evidence of what will probably go down as one of the greatest crimes in our lifetimes."[75] A PIPA-Knowledge Networks poll that same month found that 56 percent of Americans already had been convinced that "genocide" was occurring in Darfur; 69 percent also believed that, "If the UN were to determine that genocide is occurring in Darfur, then the UN, including the U.S., should decide to act to stop the genocide even if it requires military force."[76]

As the signature Nefarious bloodbath of the early twenty-first century, Darfur has been so successfully framed as "genocide" that in its December 2008 report, the Genocide Prevention Task Force singled out the "striking level of public engagement in the Darfur crisis" as a model for how to "build a permanent constituency for the prevention of genocide and mass atrocities"[77]— a statement we take to mean that the U.S. establishment's handling of the western Sudan (ca. 2003–2010) should serve as a model for how best to propagandize a conflict as "genocide," and thus to mobilize elite and public opinion for action against its alleged perpetrator.

Yet, for twice as many years as Darfur, the Democratic Republic of Congo has suffered nearly twenty times as many deaths, leading researchers to call it the "world's deadliest crisis since World War II," with an estimated 5.4 million deaths from August 1998 through April 2007.[78] But Kinshasa is not Islamic, and its foreign exploiters are the United States, Britain, France, and other African states allied with the West—most notably

Rwanda and Uganda. Hence, it is the Congo's vastly greater death toll over ten years that has been truly ignored, while to its north, it was Darfur that became a *"cause célèbre* in America," with more NGO, celebrity, student, and Internet-based activism and emotional tourism devoted to Darfur than to any other crisis in the contemporary period. The U.S. authors Steven Fake and Kevin Funk write that unlike "[e]fforts to halt Western-backed humanitarian catastrophes, such as the bloodbath in Iraq, or the Israeli Occupation, [which] fail to attract corporate funding or sympathetic pledges from the Oval Office," Darfur activism thrives because it is "largely rooted in establishment-friendly ideals such as a Western 'purity of arms', disregarding prospects for a negotiated settlement in favor of the language of force, and the use of force in this case by self-designated benevolent Westerners to save dark-skinned victims from their Arab and Muslim tormentors."[79] Given these variables, the campaign to stop the monumental bloodletting in the Congo can wait, and blood can keep flowing in Iraq, Afghanistan, Pakistan, and Palestine with fewer interruptions.

"As of today, I would not say there is a war going on in Darfur," the Nigerian General Martin Agwai, retiring as military commander of the joint UN–African Union Mission in Darfur, told reporters in late August 2009. "Militarily there is not much. What you have is security issues more now. Banditry . . . people trying to resolve issues over water and land at a local level. But real war as such, I think we are over that."[80] The *New York Times*'s coverage of Agwai's remarks reported that he had said the "war in Darfur was essentially over."[81] "Agwai became the latest senior figure . . . to play down the level of violence in Darfur," Reuters added, "where the conflict has mobilised activists who accuse Khartoum of genocide."

As news of Agwai's remarks circulated, the Save Darfur coalition immediately rejected them, as did others. Agwai "undermines international urgency in resolving these problems if people are led to believe that the war in Darfur is over," former International Crisis Group member and veteran Darfur"genocide" activist John Prendergast said, and thus "takes the wind out of the sails of international action."[82] Prendergast's Enough Project (co-founded by Prendergast in 2007 "to build a permanent constituency to prevent genocide and crimes against humanity"[83]) was just then launching a new advocacy campaign around Darfur called Keep the Promise: Sudan Now; the new campaign involved like-minded organizations such as Stop Genocide Now, the Genocide Intervention Network, and Investors Against Genocide.[84] Citing Prendergast's reaction, Alex de Waal, among the most highly respected Sudan experts in the world, was outraged. "[Prendergast's] campaign is not about domestic solutions but international (read: U.S.) action," de Waal wrote on his *Making Sense of Darfur* blog. "A campaign focused on a genocide that isn't happening, for the U.S. to step up its pressure to stop killing that has already ended, is just making Save Darfur look poorly-informed, and America look silly. . . . 'Save Darfur' isn't about Sudan, or indeed Darfur, at all—it's about an imagined empathy and generating a domestic American political agenda. Shame on you, Prendergast and your fellow 'activists,' shame, shame, shame."[85]

But Western officials, Kofi Annan's United Nations, Non-Governmental Organizations (NGOs), "human rights" celebrities, and the news media long ago succeeded in framing the crisis in Darfur as "genocide," pitting Muslim Arab perpetrators against black victims—and making it the Nefarious genocide-of-choice. This channeling of interests and emotions toward Darfur is also a wonderful diversion from the more directly Western-controlled violence in Afghanistan, Iraq, the Gaza Strip, and elsewhere. As we show throughout this book, this is the standard operating procedure for all atrocities-management campaigns.

2. BOSNIA AND HERZEGOVINA

During the civil wars that accompanied the dismantling of the Federal Republic of Yugoslavia in the 1990s, the United States, Germany, NATO, and the European Union (EU) all sided with the national groups seeking to break away from the unified federal state, and opposed the national group that held out for the longest time to preserve it, the Serbs; this placed the Western bloc solidly behind the Croats and Slovenes, then the Bosnian Muslims, and finally the Kosovo Albanians.[86]

The wars in Bosnia and Herzegovina (1992–1995) and Kosovo (1998–1999) received enormous attention in the United States and in the West generally, helped along by the creation of the ICTY and its determined service on behalf of NATO and its Yugoslavian clients (the Bosnian Muslims, Croatians, and Kosovo Albanians) and in opposition to the demonized Serbs. Because the wars were supported and even carried out by the NATO powers, and there was significant ethnic cleansing and ethnic killings, it goes almost without saying that not only "ethnic cleansing" but also the words "massacre" and "genocide" were quickly applied to Serb operations. The remarkable inflation of claims of Serb evil and violence (and playing down of NATO clients' violence), with fabricated "concentration camps," "rape camps," and similar Nazi- and Auschwitz-like analogies, caused the onetime head of the U.S. intelligence section in Sarajevo, Lieutenant Colonel John Sray, to go public even before the end of the wars in Bosnia with his claim that "America has not been so pathetically deceived since Robert McNamara helped to micromanage and escalate the Vietnam War. . . . Popular perceptions pertaining to the Bosnian Muslim government . . . have been forged by a prolific propaganda machine. A strange combination of three major spin doctors, including public relations (PR) firms in the employ of the Bosniacs, media pundits, and sympathetic elements of the US State Department, have managed to manipulate illusions to further Muslim goals."[87]

The Bosnian Muslim leadership had started touting claims of 200,000 deaths by early 1993,[88] only some nine months after the start of these civil wars, and figures such as this and 250,000 (and sometimes higher) quickly became institutionalized in the establishment media, helping to push the "genocide" claim and to justify calls for foreign intervention to protect the Bosnian Muslims. But this claim came to grief in 2005–2007, when two different studies, the first sponsored by the ICTY itself and the other by the Norwegian government, concluded that the Bosnian conflicts had resulted in combined deaths on the order of one hundred thousand for *all* sides, including both civilians and military victims.[89] Given their sources, these findings could not easily be ridiculed as "Holocaust denial" or "revisionism," but they were treated in very low key in the Western media, only slowly displacing the much higher 200,000–250,000 figures— and with no analyses and explanations of the earlier gullible acceptance of the implausible and unverified Bosnian Muslim propaganda claims.

Of course, the "Srebrenica massacre" of July 1995 has been cited heavily and repeated endlessly, and with the greatest indignation, to demonstrate that "genocide" actually had taken place in Bosnia. This was helped along by the fact that both the ICTY Trial Judgment and Decision on Appeal in the case of the Bosnian Serb General Radislav Krstic argued that genocide could occur in one "small geographical area" (the town of Srebrenica), even one where the villainous party had taken the trouble to bus all the women, children, and the elderly men to safety—that is, incontestably had not killed any but "Bosnian Muslim men of military age."[90] As Michael Mandel observes, "Genocide was transformed in this judgment, not into mere ethnic cleansing but into the killing of potential fighters during a war for military advantage. . . . In the Krstic case, the concept of genocide, except as pure propaganda, lost all contact with the Holocaust—a program for the extermination of a whole peo-

ple."[91] The case for eight thousand "men and boys" being executed at Srebrenica is extremely thin, resting in good part on the
difficulty in separating executions from battle killings (of which
there were many in the July 1995 Srebrenica actions), partly on
highly contestable witness evidence (much under coercive plea
bargaining[92]), and an interest and passionate will-to-believe the
worst of the thoroughly demonized Serbs. A videotape of
Bosnian Serbs killing six Bosnian Muslim men, far from
Srebrenica and of dubious provenance, was read even by
respectable Western analysts as serious evidence that eight thousand had been executed at Srebrenica.[93]

But even if an event such as the Srebrenica massacre occurred
exactly as accepted by the Western establishment, we are still faced
with the anomaly that the total number of deaths in Bosnia (one
hundred thousand on all sides), and even more so the number of
Bosnian Muslim civilian deaths during the four years of "genocide"
(some thirty-three thousand in all), pales into relative insignifi-
cance when compared to the deaths suffered by Iraqi civilians during the thirteen-year-long "sanctions of mass destruction" and the
now seven-year-long U.S. invasion and occupation. Given the
800,000 and one million death estimates for the two Iraqi cases,
deaths there exceeded the Bosnian Muslim civilian death toll by
24-to-1 and 30-to-1, respectively. However, as Table 1 shows, the
use of the word "genocide" was greater for Bosnia by six times for
the sanction-deaths and thirty-seven times for deaths during the
invasion-occupation. The anomaly of disparate word usage (and
differential attention and indignation) can only be explained by
the adaptation of the media and intellectuals to the propaganda
and public relations needs of the Western political establishment.
They are very attentive to and passionate about Nefarious, hence
"genocidal," bloodbaths; but they are exceedingly quiet over those
that are Constructive and display "complexities."

3. KOSOVO

In the Kosovo case as well, Western plans for attacking and dismantling Yugoslavia called for the prior demonization of the Serbs, inflating their killings of worthy victims, and preparing— *ex ante* and *ex post* justification—for the NATO bombing war, occupation, and neocolonial control of Kosovo. The ICTY played a key role in this process, having been organized from the beginning as a faux-judicial instrument of NATO's policy, which required war for its consummation, along with the indictment and prosecution of NATO's primary targets. This was the true "joint criminal enterprise" in the Balkan wars, blamed in Orwellian fashion on an alleged Serb-based "joint criminal enterprise."[94]

Just as the word "genocide" was used lavishly for the Bosnian Serbs' conduct during the wars in Bosnia, so it was applied often to the Serbs' conduct in Kosovo (i.e., inside the Republic of Serbia), both before the NATO bombing war of March 24–June 10, 1999, and during and after that war. In the year before the bombing war, as NATO prepared for the attack, the ICTY also turned its focus on Serb maltreatment of the Kosovo Albanians,[95] and Western officials, the ICTY, and Western media built up a steady volume of accusations and publicity about Serb wrongdoing. There is solid evidence that in this period the Kosovo Liberation Army (KLA) was being supplied and trained for military action by U.S. forces and was made extremely aware that provocations of the Serbs would pay off with a long prepared U.S. and NATO attack.[96] Amusingly, British Defense Secretary George Robertson acknowledged to his Parliament on the very day that NATO launched its war that, through January 1999, more people had been killed in Kosovo by the KLA than by the Serbs;[97] the total estimated killings in Kosovo since the start of 1998 were two thousand, with perhaps five hundred attributable to the Serb military.[98]

The bombing war led to some furious military action by the Serb army and the KLA in Kosovo, with many killings and a massive flight of the province's residents, Serb and Roma as well as Kosovo Albanians.[99] There were indignant official claims in the United States, Germany, and Britain of massive Serb killings and an ongoing genocide. Within days of the start of NATO's war, German Defense Minister Rudolf Scharping claimed "Genocide is starting here," and NATO spokesperson Jamie Shea that "we are now on the brink of a major humanitarian disaster . . . the likes of which we have not seen in Europe since the closing days of World War II."[100] Hysterical NATO and KLA estimates of the missing and presumably slaughtered Kosovo Albanians at times ran upwards of one hundred thousand, reaching 500,000 in one State Department press release.[101] German officials leaked "intelligence" about an alleged Serb plan called Operation Horseshoe to depopulate the province of it ethnic Albanians, and to resettle it with Serbs, which turned out to be an intelligence fabrication. KLA commander Hashim Thaci warned a German television channel that the Serbs had rounded up one hundred thousand ethnic Albanians in a soccer stadium in Pristina, their fate unknown but likely sealed. Again a piece of disinformation, but reported as probable fact. U.S. Defense Secretary William Cohen told CBS TV's *Face the Nation* program that Milosevic "put about a million and a half people out of their homes, and we're now seeing about 100,000 military-age men missing."[102]

Wartime propaganda was sustained for the first few months after the war, as forensic experts and media representatives descended on Kosovo like hungry locusts, looking for bodies and stories of massacres.[103] The search for stories ran aground on a sea of unprovable allegations and provable lies. But the *coup de grace* for the Kosovo "genocide" was the absence of bodies. In the end, only some four thousand bodies were found, including Serbs and military personnel; and by the middle of 2007, only 2,047 were still listed as missing.[104]Looking at Table 1, we can see that newspapers used the word "genocide" to apply to Serb actions in Kosovo 323 times, versus 80 for Iraq's "sanctions of mass destruction" and thirteen for the Iraq invasion-occupation, whereas the death-tolls in the last two cases exceeded that in Kosovo by 200 and 250 times. Bias could hardly be more spectacular. But you may be sure that officials, the media, and the humanitarian intellectuals have never apologized for their lies and body-count inflations or explained how all of this happened.

4. RWANDA AND THE DEMOCRATIC REPUBLIC OF CONGO

Elsewhere we have written that the breakup of Yugoslavia "may have been the most misrepresented series of major events over the past twenty years."[105] But the far bloodier and destructive invasions, insurgencies, and civil wars that have ravaged several countries in the Great Lakes region of Central Africa over the same years may have been subjected to even greater misrepresentation.

To a remarkable degree, all major sectors of the Western establishment swallowed a propaganda line on Rwanda that turned perpetrator and victim upside-down. In the much-cited 1999 study of "Genocide in Rwanda" on behalf of Human Rights Watch and the International Federation of Human Rights in Paris, Alison Des Forges writes that "By late March 1994, Hutu Power leaders were determined to slaughter massive numbers of Tutsi and Hutu opposed to [Hutu President Juvénal] Habyarimana," and that on April 6, 1994, with the assassination of Habyarimana, "A small group of his close associates . . . decided to execute the planned extermination." Although "responsibility for killing Habyarimana is a serious issue," it pales in comparison to "responsibility for the genocide. We know little about who assassinated Habyarimana"—a false statement, as shown below—but "We know more about who used the assassination as the pretext to begin a slaughter that had been planned for months"—true enough, but in exactly the opposite sense reported by Des Forges.[106]

During testimony at a major trial of four Hutu former military officers before the International Criminal Tribunal for Rwanda (ICTR), Des Forges acknowledged that by April 1992 (i.e., a full twenty-four months before "the genocide" is alleged to have been implemented), the "government in charge of Rwanda [had become] a multiparty government, including Tutsi representatives, and it is for that reason alone that it is impossible to conclude that there was planning of a genocide by that government."[107] Although Des Forges tried to salvage the Hutu conspiracy model, alleging plans by individual Hutu members of the coalition government to use their "official powers" to carry out a preplanned genocide, this model disintegrated on cross-examination.[108] Des Forges could not explain how Hutu "individuals" used these "powers" without the knowledge of their Tutsi and Rwandan Patriotic Front (RPF) associates. Furthermore, she was forced to admit that pro-RPF ministers were in cahoots with the RPF and its plans for war (which we describe below) and that after the Habyarimana assassination, the RPF did not simply respond in self-defense to a Hutu-organized killing spree, but initiated its own killing spree. In other words, while the Hutu members of Rwanda's power-sharing government couldn't possibly have planned a genocide against the Tutsi, the Tutsi-led RPF was well-positioned to paralyze any government response to plans it had developed—and that were implemented—to avoid the threat of a free election the RPF was destined to lose, to assassinate the Hutu president, and to take over the country by military force. Yet, Des Forges' dramatic concessions before the ICTR never turned up in the Western media, and in her public statements thereafter she continued to repeat the official propaganda line about a Hutu conspiracy to commit genocide right up to the very end.[109]

To accept the standard model of "The Genocide," one must ignore the large-scale killing and ethnic cleansing of Hutus by the RPF long before the April-July 1994 period, which began when Ugandan forces invaded Rwanda under President (and dictator) Yoweri Museveni on October 1, 1990. At its inception, the RPF was a wing of the Ugandan army, with the RPF's leader, Paul Kagame, having served as director of Ugandan military intelligence in the 1980s. The Ugandan invasion and resultant combat were not a "civil war," but rather a clear case of *aggression*. Yet this led to no reprimand or cessation of support by the United States or Britain—and in contrast to Iraq's invasion of Kuwait just two months before, which was countered in the Security Council by the same-day demand that Iraq withdraw its forces immediately, the Council took no action on the Ugandan invasion of Rwanda until March 1993 and did not even authorize an observer mission (UNOMUR) until late June 1993; the RPF by then occupied much of northern Rwanda and had driven out several hundred thousand Hutu farmers.[110]

It is clear that Museveni and the RPF were perceived as serving U.S. interests and that the government of President Habyarimana was targeted for ouster.[111] UN Security Council inaction flowed from this political bias. In his assessment of the years he spent representing U.S. interests in Africa, former Assistant Secretary of State Herman Cohen raised the question of why, as of October 1, 1990, the "first day of the crisis," as he calls it, "did [the United States] automatically exclude the policy option of informing Ugandan President Museveni that the invasion of Rwanda by uniformed members of the Ugandan army was totally unacceptable, and that the continuation of good relations between the United States and Uganda would depend on his getting the RPF back across the border?"[112] This is naive but revealing—the answer, like that to the question of why the United States lobbied for the withdrawal of UN forces from Rwanda as the "genocide" was getting underway in April 1994, is that the

Ugandan army and RPF were doing what the United States wanted done in Rwanda.

The United States and its allies worked hard in the early 1990s to weaken the Rwandan government, forcing the abandonment of many of the economic and social gains from the social revolution of 1959, and thereby making the Habyarimana government less popular and helping to reinforce the Tutsi minority's economic power.[113] Eventually, the RPF was able to achieve a legal military presence inside Rwanda thanks to a series of ceasefires and other agreements that led to the Arusha Peace Accords of August 1993. Pressed upon the Rwandan government by the United States and its allies, they called for the "integration" of the armed forces of Rwanda and the RPF and for a "transitional," power-sharing government until national elections could be held in 1995.[114] These accords positioned the RPF for its bloody overthrow of a relatively democratic coalition government and the takeover of the Rwandan state by a minority dictatorship.

As we have already suggested, the established perpetrator-victim line requires suppression of the crucial fact that the shooting-down of the government jet returning Rwandan President Juvénal Habyarimana and Burundian President Cyprien Ntaryamira to Kigali on April 6, killing everyone on board, was carried out by RPF commandos and had been regarded by RPF planners as an essential first strike in its final assault on the government. Although the mass killings *followed* this assassination, with the RPF rapidly defeating any military resistance by the successor to Habyarimana's coalition government and establishing its rule in Rwanda, these prime *génocidaires* were and still are today portrayed as heroic defenders of Rwanda's national unity against Hutu "extremists" and the *Interahamwe* militia, the RPF's actual victims.

Acceptance of this line also requires the suppression of a key verdict in a December 2008 *Judgment* by the ICTR.[115] This seven-and-a-half-year trial of four former high-ranking Hutu members of the Rwanda military produced an acquittal of all four defendants on the Tribunal's most serious charge: That they participated in an alleged conspiracy to commit genocide against the country's Tutsi minority. To the contrary, the court ruled unanimously that the evidence is "consistent with preparations for a political or military power struggle and measures adopted in the context of an ongoing war with the RPF that were used for other purposes from 6 April 1994."[116] Of course, it was the RPF that had been organized to carry out a "military power struggle" against Rwanda's Hutu majority for several years prior to April 1994; and with its Tutsi base a numerical minority in the country (at most 15 percent overall), the RPF recognized that they would suffer an almost certain defeat in the free elections called for by the Arusha Accords. But that it was the RPF, itself, that conspired to assassinate Habyarimana and to carry out subsequent mass killings in its aftermath remains entirely beyond the grasp of the ICTR. Although it has failed to convict a single Hutu of the conspiracy to commit genocide charge, the ICTR has never once entertained the question of an *RPF conspiracy*— despite the RPF's rapid overthrow of the Hutu government and capture of the Rwandan state. This, we believe, flows from U.S. and allied support of the RPF, reflected in media coverage, humanitarian intellectuals' and NGO activism, as well as the ICTR's jurisprudence.

Paul Kagame and the RPF were creatures of U.S. power from their origins in Uganda in the 1980s. Allan Stam, a Rwanda scholar who once served with the U.S. Army Special Forces, notes that Kagame "had spent some time at Fort Leavenworth, . . . not too far before the 1994 genocide." Fort Leavenworth is the U.S. Army's "commander general staff college, . . . where rising stars of the U.S. military and other places go to get training as they are on track to become generals. The training that they get there is on planning large-scale operations. It's not planning small-scale logistic things. It's not tactics. It's about how do you plan an invasion. And apparently [Kagame] did very well." By 1994, Kagame's RPF possessed a sophisticated plan for seizing power in Rwanda that, in its final execution, Stam says, "looks staggeringly like the United States' invasion of Iraq in 1991," as well as the manpower and the materiel necessary to carry it out. Stam adds that the RPF launched its final assault on the Rwandan government almost immediately after the assassination of Habyarimana, within 60 to 120 minutes of the shooting-down of his jet, with "50,000 [RPF] soldiers mov[ing] into action on two fronts, in a coordinated fashion"—clearly "a plan that was not worked out on the back of an envelope."[117]

So the Hutu conspiracy model, still at the center of establishment belief even if implicitly rejected by the ICTR, suffers from the RPF-Kagame locus of responsibility for the triggering event (the shoot-down of Habyarimana's jet during its approach to Kigali airport) and the incredible speed and coordinated nature of the RPF's military response, which again suggest detailed planning, and a different set of conspirators.

But there is also the fact that the alleged Hutu perpetrators of "The Genocide" were the ones *driven from power*, with several million Hutus sent fleeing from Rwanda by July 4, the date by which the RPF had taken Kigali. We also see that before the end of July, Washington withdrew diplomatic recognition from the ousted government and awarded it to the RPF—the "entity that exercises effective control in Rwanda," a State Department spokesman explained. And we see that at the same time, Washington began dispatching U.S. troops and large-scale aid to Kigali,[118] after having lobbied and voted at the Security Council on April 21 for a withdrawal of virtually all UN troops, over the objections of Rwanda's ambassador,[119] positively facilitating both the slaughters and the RPF's conquest of power. If the established narrative about "who used the assassination as a pretext" were true, then Rwanda would be the first case in history in which a minority population, suffering destruction at the hands of its tormentors, drove its tormentors from power and assumed control of a country, all in the span of less than one hundred days. We find this incredible in the extreme.

So does a whole body of important but suppressed research. An investigation in July and August 1994, sponsored by the UN High Commissioner for Refugees (UNHCR) to document Hutu massacres of Tutsis, found instead massacres of Hutu civilians in RPF-controlled areas of Rwanda on the order of twenty-five to forty-five thousand, leading the UNHCR to take the extraordinary step of blocking Hutu refugees from returning to Rwanda in order to protect them. Prepared by Robert Gersony, the report "concluded that there was 'an unmistakable pattern of killings and persecutions' by soldiers of the [RPF] . . . 'aimed at Hutu populations,'" the *New York Times* reported. But the Gersony report "set off a bitter dispute within the world organization and led the Secretary General to demand that the United Nations officials refrain from discussing it," in an effort to placate the RPF and, more importantly, its Western sponsors.[120] Officially, the report "does not exist" at the United Nations,[121] and Gersony was instructed never to discuss his findings (a ban he has largely respected[122]).

A memorandum drafted in September 1994 for the eyes of Secretary of State Warren Christopher reported that the UNHCR team "concluded that a pattern of killing had emerged" in Rwanda, the "[RPF] and Tutsi civilian surrogates [killing] 10,000 or more Hutu civilians per month, with the [RPF] accounting for 95% of the killing." This memorandum added that "the UNHR team speculated that the purpose of the killing was a campaign of ethnic cleansing intended to clear certain areas in the south of Rwanda for Tutsi habitation. The killings also served to reduce the population of Hutu males and discourages refugees from returning to claim their lands."[123] The added significance of this campaign was that the south of Rwanda shares a border with northern Burundi, where a majority Tutsi population long has dwelled.

Separately, U.S. academics Christian Davenport and Allan Stam estimated that more than one million deaths occurred in Rwanda from April through July 1994.[124] They concluded that the "majority of victims were likely Hutu and not Tutsi." Initially sponsored by the ICTR, but later dropped by it, Davenport and Stam's work shows convincingly that the theaters where the killing was greatest correlated with spikes in RPF activity (i.e., with RFP "surges," in their terminology), as a series of RPF advances, particularly in the month of April 1994, created roving patterns of killing. In fact, they describe at least seven distinct "surges" by the RFP (e.g., "they surged forward from the North downward into the Northwest and middle-eastern part of the country"), and every time, an RPF "surge" was accompanied by serious local bloodbaths.[125] Then in late 2009, Davenport and Stam reported what they called the "most shocking result" of their research to date: "The killings in the zone controlled by the FAR [i.e., the Hutu-controlled Armed Forces of Rwanda] seemed to escalate as the RPF moved into the country and acquired more territory. When the RPF advanced, large-scale killings escalated. When the RPF stopped, large-scale killings largely decreased."[126]

With these facts, Davenport and Stam appear to link the mass killings of 1994 to RPF actions; this work also suggests that the mass killings were not directed against the Tutsi population. Moreover, a number of observers as well as participants in the events of 1994 claim that the great majority of deaths were Hutu, with some estimates as high as two million.[127]

Yet, Davenport and Stam shy away from asserting the most important lesson of their work—not only that the majority of killings took place in those theaters where the RPF "surged," but also that the RPF was the only well-organized killing force within Rwanda in 1994, and the only one that planned a major military offensive.[128] Clearly, the chief responsibility for Rwandan political violence belonged to the RPF, and not to the ousted coalition government, the FAR, or any Hutu-related group. But Davenport and

Stam are inconsistent on the question of likely perpetrators, with their evidence of likely RPF responsibility contradicted by assertions of primary responsibility on the part of the FAR.[129] In short, their work does not break away from the mainstream camp overall. However, they do acknowledge that forms of political violence took place other than a straightforward Hutu "genocide" against the minority Tutsi—in itself, a rarity in Western circles. As with the suppressed Gersony report, Davenport and Stam's findings caused great dismay at the United Nations, not to mention in Washington and Kigali. They have been under attack and in retreat since they were expelled from Rwanda in November 2003, when they first reported that the "majority of the victims of 1994 were of the same ethnicity as the government in power," and have been barred from entering the country ever since.[130] The established narrative's 800,000 or more largely Tutsi deaths resulting from a "preprogrammed genocide" committed by "Hutu Power" appears to have no basis in any facts beyond the early claims by Kagame's RPF and its politically motivated Western sponsors and propagandists.

We also know a lot more about "who assassinated Habyarimana." In one of the most important, and also suppressed, stories about "The Genocide," former ICTR investigator Michael Hourigan developed evidence as far back as 1996–1997, based on the testimony of three RPF informants who claimed "direct involvement in the 1994 fatal rocket attack upon the President's aircraft" and "specifically implicated the direct involvement of [Kagame]" and other members of the RPF. But in early 1997, when Hourigan hand-delivered his evidence to the ICTR's chief prosecutor, Louise Arbour, the latter was "aggressive" and "hostile," Hourigan recounts in a 2006 affidavit,[131] and advised him that the "investigation was at an end because in her view it was not in [the ICTR's] mandate"—a decision that "astounded" Hourigan. It is one that former ICTR chief prosecutor Richard Goldstone also rejected, telling a Danish newspaper that the assassination is "clearly related to the genocide," as it was the "trigger that started the genocide. . . ."[132] Suppressing evidence of the assassination's perpetrator has been crucial in the West, as it seems awkward that the "trigger" for "The Genocide" was ultimately pulled, not by the officially-designated Hutu villains, but by the Tutsi victors in this conflict, the RPF, long supported by the United States and by its close allies (who very possibly aided the assassins in the shoot-down[133]). It has also been important to suppress the fact that the first Hutu president of Burundi, Melchior Ndadaye, had been assassinated by Tutsi officers of his army in October 1993, an action celebrated by the RPF and stirring fears among Rwanda's Hutus.

A far more comprehensive eight-year investigation by the French magistrate Jean-Louis Bruguière, who had been asked to rule on the deaths of the three French nationals operating the government jet that was shot down in April 1994, concluded that the assassination followed from Kagame's rejection of the Arusha power-sharing accords of August 1993, and that for Kagame the "physical elimination" of Habyarimana was therefore essential to achieving the goal of an RPF takeover in Rwanda.[134] Bruguière issued nine arrest warrants for high-ranking RPF members close to Kagame and requested that the ICTR, itself, take up Kagame's prosecution, as under French law, Bruguière could not issue an arrest warrant for a head of state.[135]

As best we can tell, the existence of Hourigan's evidence has been reported only once in two different U.S. newspapers (the *Los Angeles Times* and *Seattle Times*), and never in the *New York Times*, *Washington Post*, or *Wall Street Journal*; Bruguière's findings were mentioned in several U.S. newspapers (sixteen that we have found), including three short items in the *Washington Post*, a major report in the *Los Angeles Times* (reprinted in the *Seattle Times*), and one blurb apiece in the *New York Times* and *Wall Street Journal* totaling ninety-four words.[136] Amusingly, the U.S. media have reported fairly often on Bruguière's work as a "counterterrorism" specialist in France, including several dozen items in the *New York Times*, *Washington Post*, and *Wall Street Journal*. But when we check the U.S. media for Bruguière's eight-year inquiry into mass killing in Rwanda, a case where his focus was on a U.S. client-agent as the primary villain, their interest declines close to *zero*.[137] The propaganda system works.

The invasions, assassinations, and mass slaughters by which the RPF shot its way to power in Kigali advanced many objectives, and their support by the "enlightened" states is regarded by many of the defense teams that practice before the ICTR as reflecting a *quid pro quo* between Washington and the RPF: Washington gains a strong military presence in Central Africa, a diminution of its European rivals' influence, proxy armies to serve its interests, and access to the raw material-rich Democratic Republic of Congo; the RPF renews Tutsi-minority control of Rwanda and gains a free hand to kill any perceived internal rivals, along with a client state's usual immunities, money, weapons, foreign investment, and a great deal of international prestige.

One year after ICTY and ICTR chief prosecutor Carla Del Ponte (successor to Louise Arbour) opened what she called the "Special Investigation" of the RPF in 2002, she was terminated as chief prosecutor at the ICTR, despite taking her plea directly to Secretary-General Kofi Annan, whom Del Ponte called inflexible on the question. In her memoirs, Del Ponte recounts a June 2002 meeting with Kagame at his presidential abode in Kigali. Kagame, "fuming," told her: "If you investigate [the RPF], people will believe there were two genocides. . . . All we did was liberate Rwanda." This was followed by a May 2003 meeting with Pierre Prosper, the Bush administration's ambassador-at-large for war crimes, who, in Del Ponte's words, "backed the Rwandans" and "suggested that [she] surrender responsibility for investigating and prosecuting the alleged crimes of the RPF." By the time Del Ponte was able to meet with Annan in New York in late July 2003, she told Annan: "This will be the end of the Special Investigation," and to which Annan replied: "Yes. I know."[138]

Del Ponte told an interviewer after her position with the ICTR ended: "It is clear that it all started when we embarked on these Special Investigations" and "pressure from Rwanda contributed to the non-renewal of my mandate."[139] Doubtless, pressure from other sources with a lot more clout on the Security Council played an even greater role. Former ICTR (and ICTY) spokesperson Florence Hartmann also recounts extensive interference by the United States, Britain, and Kagame's RPF in every effort by the Office of the Prosecutor to investigate RPF crimes.[140] Hassan Jallow, Del Ponte's successor at the ICTR, has stated on the record that he does not believe the assassination of Habyarimana belongs within the ICTR's mandate, and under his charge (September 2003 on) the Office of the Prosecutor systematically dragged its feet when it came to the crimes of the RPF, always pleading a need to carry out "additional inquiries" without ever bringing a single indictment.[141] Through the end of 2008, 100 percent of the ICTR's indictments for "serious violations of international humanitarian law" committed during 1994 have been brought against Hutu members of the former government and ethnic Hutus more generally, and none against members of the RPF, despite the ICTR's Statute making no distinctions on the basis of ethnicity or political allegiance.[142] Neither the RPF's violent takeover of Rwanda, its massacre of "10,000 or more Hutu civilians" per month in 1994, nor any of its other numerous post-war slaughters, have ever once been disturbed by criminal charges at the ICTR.

Very big lies about Rwanda are now institutionalized and are part of the common (mis)understanding in the West. In reality, Rwanda's Paul Kagame is one of the great mass murderers of our time. Yet, thanks to the remarkable myth structure that surrounds him, he enjoys immense popularity with his chief patron in Washington, the image of this big-time killer transmuted into that of an honored savior deserving strong Western support. Philip Gourevitch, one of Kagame's prime apologists for many years, portrays him as an emancipator, a "man of action with an acute human and political intelligence" who "made things happen"; he also compares Kagame to "another famously tall and skinny civil warrior, Abraham Lincoln."[143] A more recent hagiography by Stephen Kinzer portrays Kagame as the founding father of a New Africa. It is "one of the most amazing untold stories of the modern history of revolution," as Kinzer explains it, because Kagame overthrew a dictatorship, stopped a genocide, and turned Rwanda into "one of the great stars" of the continent, with Western investment and favorable PR flowing.[144] In fact, what Kagame overthrew was a multiethnic, power-sharing, coalition government; what Kagame imposed was a Tutsi-dominated dictatorship; and what Kagame turned Rwanda and the whole of Central Africa into was a rolling genocide that is still ongoing— but it is true that he is a shining "star" in the Western firmament and its propaganda system.

In Samantha Power's view, and in accord with this same myth structure, "The United States did almost nothing to try to stop [the Hutu genocide]," but instead "stood on the sidelines"— "bystanders to genocide."[145] But this is doubly false. What the United States and its Western allies (Britain, Canada, and Belgium) really did was sponsor the U.S.-trained Kagame, support his invasion of Rwanda from Uganda and the massive ethnic cleansing prior to April 1994, weaken the Rwandan state by forcing an economic recession and the RPF's penetration of the government and throughout the country, and then press for the complete removal of UN troops because they didn't want UN troops to stand in the way of Kagame's conquest of the country, even though Rwanda's Hutu authorities were urging the dispatch of *more* UN troops.[146] Former UN Secretary-General Boutros Boutros-Ghali also wanted to increase UN troop strength,[147] and complained bitterly in his memoirs about the "obstruction" caused by the Clinton administration: "The U.S. effort to prevent the effective deployment of a UN force for Rwanda succeeded,

with the strong support of Britain," he wrote; the Security
Council "meekly followed the United States' lead. . . ."[148] (We
may recall that Samantha Power also claimed that the United
States "looked away" when Indonesia invaded East Timor in
1975, when in fact the U.S. gave Indonesia the go-ahead, the arms
to carry out the invasion, and diplomatic protection in the United
Nations. For Power, whenever the United States colludes in a
genocidal process, she pretends that U.S. guilt is at worst that of
remaining a mere "bystander," but never that of an accomplice, let
alone a perpetrator.)

In the Rwanda "genocide" case, the "human rights" community played an unusually active role in supporting the real aggressors and killers, in close parallel with their own governments' per-
spectives and policies. As in the case of the Western aggressions
against Yugoslavia (1999) and Iraq (2003), Human Rights Watch
and other nongovernmental organizations simply ignored the
"supreme international crime" (or "act of aggression by Uganda,"
in Herman Cohen's phrase) while conveniently, and in hugely
biased fashion, featuring lesser human rights violations.[149] They
downplayed or ignored entirely the refugee crisis created by the
Ugandan-RPF invasion and occupation of northern Rwanda and
the armed penetration and *de facto* subversion of the rest of the
country by the RPF. Every response to these by the Habyarimana
government from October 1990 onward was scrutinized for
"human rights" violations and framed as evidence of unlawful state
repression. They systematically evaded the massive evidence of
RPF responsibility for the April 6, 1994, shoot-down surely
because the finding conflicts with their deep commitment to the
model of a preplanned Hutu genocide and the RPF's self-defen-
sive rescue of Rwanda, the twin components of the established
perpetrator-victim line. We believe that their biases played an
important role in supporting the RPF's aggression, its penetration
of the country, and the execution of its final assault on power.
Above all, we believe that their biases and propaganda service con-

tributed substantially to the mass killings that followed—all in accord with the needs of actual U.S. policy.

On March 8, 1993, just days before the Security Council took up the situation in Rwanda for the first time, a consortium of four human rights organizations, led by Human Rights Watch and calling itself the International Commission of Inquiry into Human Rights Abuses in Rwanda, issued its report.[150] The commission concluded that, rather than Rwanda having suffered an invasion by Uganda, from which the Habyarimana government had yet to liberate its country, the Habyarimana government was instead guilty of something very close to a genocidal rampage against the country's Tutsi minority, with two thousand dead since October 1990, "systematic killings," widespread rape, and a "climate of terror."[151] Alison Des Forges, one of the commission's co-chairs, later commented that this report "put Rwandan human rights abuses squarely before the international community"[152]— but it was only the Habyarimana government's alleged abuses that the commission focused on.

The commission produced its report after its members spent no more than two weeks on the ground in Rwanda in January of that year and only two hours in territory controlled by the RPF. The commission itself had close ties to the RPF, its sponsors "either directly funded by the RPF or infiltrated by it," Robin Philpot reports.[153] Prior to her work on this commission, Des Forges had worked for the U.S. Department of State and National Security Council. William Schabas, a Canadian member of the commission, issued a press release at the time the full report was released that bore the title "Genocide and War Crimes in Rwanda."[154] He thus drew attention to a category of crime that not even the establishment narrative alleges was to begin for another thirteen months. Stressing that in the work of the commission the "word genocide has been mentioned on a number of occasions," Daniel Jacoby, the president of the International Federation of Human Rights League, stated that the situation in Rwanda "is not simply an ethnic confrontation. It goes beyond that. Responsibility for the killings can be placed extremely high."[155] Human Rights Watch's annual *World Report* covering 1993 noted that when the RPF launched its major offensive that year, "it justified the offensive in part by the need to counter human rights abuses of the Rwanda government" such as those put squarely before the world by the commission's report. In short, with the brunt of its findings coming down against the Habyarimana government, the commission's work served to delegitimize the government of Rwanda and enhance the legitimacy of the armed forces of the RPF. As the RPF quickly used the commission's claims to justify a new killing spree, we believe the case can be made that the overall impact of this report—and of the work of HRW and its allies with respect to Rwanda over the past two decades—was to underwrite the mass killings to follow, including the vast numbers in the Democratic Republic of Congo, regularly explained as carried out by the benevolent RPF and Uganda in search of Hutu "*génocidaires*."

As we see on Table 1 (p. 35), the 1994 mass killings in Rwanda remain the *sine qua non* for "genocide" usage, generating more attributions for this theater than for any other in our survey (3,199, nearly triple the number for Darfur). This, we believe, follows from the successful framing of the Hutus as the villains, executing a pre-planned "genocide" against the Tutsis—a Nefarious and Mythical bloodbath at one and the same time—and Kagame's RPF as the defender-savior of the Tutsis and of Rwanda and Central Africa as a whole, with the RPF unexpectedly finding itself the new power in the country one day. But it also cleared the ground for Kagame and Uganda's Yoweri Museveni—Kagame's ally and the two staunchest U.S. clients in the region—to periodically invade and occupy the DRC (named Zaire through 1997) and beyond without opposition from the "international community."

The Pentagon has very actively supported these invasions of the DRC, even more heavily than it supported the RPF's drive to take Kigali. This led to the killing of many thousands of Hutu refugees in a series of mass slaughters (*ca.* 1994–1997), and also provided cover for a greater series of Kagame-Museveni assaults on the Congo that have destabilized life in this large country of perhaps sixty million people, with literally millions perishing in the process.[156] In his letter of resignation to Chief Prosecutor Hassan Jallow, Filip Rentjens, a Dutch academic and one time expert witness before the ICTR, took issue with the "impunity" that protects the RPF leadership from prosecution. "[RPF] crimes fall squarely within the mandate of the ICTR," he wrote, and "they are well documented, testimonial and material proof is available, and the identity of the RPF suspects is known. . . . It is precisely because the regime in Kigali has been given a sense of impunity that, during the years following 1994, it has committed massive internationally recognized crimes in both Rwanda and the DRC."[157]

But this again has been compatible with Western interests and policy, as it contributed to the replacement of Mobutu with the more amenable Laurent Kabila (and later his son Joseph) and the opening up of the Congo to a new surge of ruthless exploitation of precious gems, rare industrial minerals, and timber by Western companies in a different kind of "resource war"—a fine illustration of "shock therapy" with murderous human consequences for the Congolese people, the equivalent of "one tsunami every six months" for more than a decade,[158] but with large gains to a small business and military elite. In a series of UN reports which coined the phrase "elite networks" to denote the "politically and economically powerful groups involved in the exploitation activities" that lie at the heart of the Congo genocide, we read that "The war economy controlled by the three elite networks [i.e., Kinshasa, Rwanda, and Uganda] operating in the Democratic Republic of the Congo dominates the economic activities of much of the Great Lakes region. . . . Years of lawlessness and a Government incapable of protecting its citizens have allowed the armed groups to loot and plunder the country's resources with impunity. . . . They have

Some Benign Bloodbaths

1. ISRAEL: SABRA AND SHATILA

As the leading U.S. client and recipient of foreign aid, and with extraordinary power over U.S. Middle East policy, sometimes referred to as the "tail that wags the dog," Israel enjoys great freedom in international affairs, including the privilege of threatening and even invading foreign territories, without derogatory reference, indignation, or policy constraints coming from its patron (the dog). In fact, Israel's aggressions, law violations, and blood-baths are almost always partially funded and diplomatically protected by major sectors of the U.S. establishment, from the executive and congressional branches through its news media. Like its patron, this exempts Israel from international law and the constraints of the UN Charter and "international community," and emboldens Israel to commit aggression and war crimes. It also renders Israel's actions relatively free from designation by invidious words such as "genocide," "war crimes," "ethnic cleansing" or "crimes against humanity."

Thus Israel could invade and occupy Lebanon in 1982, killing an estimated fifteen to twenty thousand Lebanese citizens and Palestinian refugees in the process, and suffer no UN Security

Council penalty or threat, or call from any humanitarian interventionists for action to protect its victims. As in the later case of Israel's invasion of Lebanon in July–August 2006, U.S.–U.K–EU, and thus UN, protection of the aggressor gave it leeway to kill without international penalty.

In a notable episode during the 1982 invasion-occupation, the high command of the Israel Defense Force (IDF) enabled the Christian Phalange militia to enter the Palestinian refugee camps at Sabra and Shatila in Muslim West Beirut on September 16, 1982, knowing full well that mass killings would follow. Established shortly after the 1948 Arab–Israeli war for the Palestinians driven from their homes in Israel at the founding of the Jewish state, these camps housed unarmed women, children, and elderly people, largely the remaining relatives of Palestinians who had fled Beirut during the prior weeks of conflict, but also some Lebanese nationals. The bloody assault on Sabra and Shatila was the culmination of a series of IDF attacks on Palestinian refugee camps (at Tyre and Sidon, for example) during its sweep northward to Beirut beginning on June 6 that had razed each refugee camp to the ground in a massive operation the IDF named "Peace for Galilee."[160]

On September 14, Bashir Gemayel, the Christian Phalangist president of Lebanon, was assassinated when a bomb destroyed much of his party's office in Christian East Beirut, where a Phalange meeting was being held. The incident "was a painful blow to Israel," the Israeli journalist Amnon Kapeliouk reported, as Gemayel "was the sworn enemy of the Palestinians," and strongly aligned with Israel.[161] Within twenty-four hours of the assassination, the IDF moved to occupy all of Muslim West Beirut, which the IDF had not entered until then. "We are going to mop-up West Beirut," IDF General Raphael Eitan told Israel's *Ma'ariv* newspaper. "We will find all the terrorists and their leaders. We will destroy whatever requires destruction." On September 15, the IDF met with top figures of the Christian

Phalange militia to "[work] out the details of the Christian militi-
amen's role in the takeover of West Beirut," Kapeliouk's account
continues. "At the end of the meeting, a Phalangist military commander admitted to the Israelis: 'We have been waiting for this
moment for many years'."162

The IDF completely surrounded the Sabra and Shatila
refugee camps and established checkpoints allowing it "to control
all entrances and exits." In the evening of September 16, the IDF
permitted the Phalange militia to enter the camps, and the "carnage began immediately," lasting "forty hours without interruption," with the IDF "able to observe the operations from the roof
(seventh floor) of the three Lebanese buildings they had occupied since September 3." By 10a.m. September 18, between eight
hundred and three thousand Palestinian civilians had been
slaughtered. As Kapeliouk summed up the massacre: "The Israeli
Army surrounded the camps, disarmed the Lebanese militias hostile to the Phalangists, coordinated the latter's entry into the
camps giving them diverse logistical support, and closed its eyes
and ears during forty hours of carnage."163

 Although this mass killing was widely reported and frequently
called a massacre—584 times in the newspapers, as shown in
Table 3164—the word "genocide" was only rarely applied to Sabra
and Shatila—only four times in the newspapers, only once in the
New York Times, in an Associated Press report quoting Yasir
Arafat,165 and never in the Washington Post. This word usage, the
generous reporting about the self-exonerating Israeli Kahan
Commission of Inquiry's treatment of the massacre,166 and the
steady media failure to look back on the event (as the media do
with Srebrenica, intensively, every July) and tie it to major Israeli
leaders like then-Defense Minister and later Prime Minister Ariel
Sharon and Israeli army General Raphael Eitan and General
Amos Yaron, who were deeply involved in the killings, made it
possible for them to prosper in Israeli politics and to gain acceptance as leaders by the "international community."

TABLE 3: Differential Use of "Massacre" and "Genocide" for Benign and Nefarious Atrocities [A]

Col. 1	Col. 2	Col. 3	Col. 4
Theater where atrocities occurred	Estimated Deaths per Theater	Use of the "Massacre" Label	Use of the "Genocide" Label
El Mozote	800–1,000	122	1
Rio Negro	444	21	0
Sabra–Shatila	800–3,000	584	4
Halabja	5,000	122	10
Two Sarajevo Marketplace Attacks	111	266	2
Srebrenica	7,000–8,000 [D]	2,327	442
Serb Krajina– Operation Storm	2,000	0	1
Racak	45	312	0
Liquica	60–200	102	0
Dasht-e-Leili	960–4,000	0	0
Falluja	4,000	29	31
Gaza Strip	1,400	72	60

[A] Factiva database searches carried out under the "Newspapers: All" category in January 2009. The exact search parameters are described in note 161. We used the database operators *w/5 massacre* and *w/10 genocid** to capture all variations of our particular search terms occurring anywhere in the title or text within five or within ten words of the other primary search term.

[B] Taking each row in turn: (1) El Mozote, El Salvador, December 11, 1981; (2) Rio Negro, Guatemala, March 13, 1982; (3) Sabra-Shatila Palestinian refugee camps, Beirut, Lebanon, September 16–18, 1982; (4) Halabja, Kurdish (Patriotic Union of Kurdistan) province of Sulaymaniyah, northeastern Iraq, March 15–16, 1988; (5) Sarajevo, Bosnia and Herzegovina, February 5, 1994 and August 28, 1995; (6) Srebrenica, eastern Bosnia and Herzegovina, July 11–20, 1995; (7) Krajina (or border) regions of Croatia and Bosnia and Herzegovina, August 1995; (8) Račak, Kosovo province, Federal Republic of Yugoslavia, January 15, 1999; (9) Liquiçá, East Timor, April 6, 1999; (10) Dasht-e-Leili, northern Afghanistan, November,

2001; (11) Falluja, Iraq, November, 2004; (12) Gaza Strip, December 27, 2008–January 18, 2009.

[C] We've reported estimated death tolls causally linked with the theater or locale named in Col. 1. Where appropriate, we acknowledge that a range of estimates is available. Note that at times the reported estimates strike us as improbable and incorrect (as well as fraudulent or *mythical*).

[D] The estimated death toll reported for Srebrenica in Table 3 is contested.

The contrast with the treatment of the Serb leadership and of ethnic Serbs more generally, whose alleged (and inflated) crimes are not as easily erased and whose "victims" must be satisfied that justice triumphs, could hardly be more dramatic. The Yugoslavia Tribunal stated that the "killing of all members of the part of a group located within a small geographical area . . . would qualify as genocide if carried out with the intent to destroy the part of the group as such located in this small geographical area."[167] In late 1982, the UN General Assembly—in contrast to the non-action by the Security Council—resolved that the Sabra-Shatila "massacre was an act of genocide."[168] You may be sure that none of this showed up in the free press.

2. ISRAEL: THE GAZA INVASION
OF DECEMBER 2008–JANUARY 2009

On December 27, 2008, Israel launched a military offensive against the Gaza Strip that from its first day on amounted to a wholesale slaughter of the Gaza Palestinians. By the date the Israel Defense Forces (IDF) announced a ceasefire effective as of January 18, approximately fourteen hundred Gazans had been killed, 850 of them civilians, and more than five thousand wounded, with women and children suffering 30 percent of the casualties. Israelis also died, ten of whom were IDF soldiers participating in the assault (three from "friendly fire"). The scale of the physical damage was immense, with three thousand houses destroyed and another eleven thousand damaged, as well as mosques, hospitals, colleges, factories, small businesses, and even United Nations property damaged or destroyed, orange and olive groves bulldozed flat, and large areas of densely crowded cities such as Gaza City left in rubble and resembling earthquake zones.[169]

"[N]owhere in Gaza was [it] safe for civilians," the Red Cross reported.[170] A fact-finding mission headed by John Dugard on behalf of the League of Arab States concluded that the "IDF had not distinguished between civilians and civilian objects and military targets."[171] Although a group of sixteen prominent jurists and human rights figures addressed an open letter to the Secretary-General in which they urged him to initiate a UN inquiry into violations of international and humanitarian law committed during the attack,[172] the Secretary-General rejected the idea—"I do not plan any further inquiry," Ban Ki-moon told the Security Council.[173] Instead, the inquiry would have to be undertaken by the Geneva-based UN Human Rights Council, which the United States rejoined in early 2009 under the new Obama administration in part to "[fight] against the anti-Israel crap,"[174] as UN Ambassador Susan Rice explained, and where the inquiry's findings and recommendations were eventually rejected by both the U.S. and E.U. delegations.

The alleged purpose of Operation Cast Lead (Israel's name for the onslaught) was to stop Hamas from firing rockets across Gaza's northern border with Israel toward Sderot and other nearby villages in southern Israel, formerly Palestinian land but ethnically cleansed and now inhabited by Jewish settlers—a bit of nasty displacement reality, in contrast with the Serbs' mythical "Operation Horseshoe," a figment of Western propaganda alleging a Serb plan to drive the ethnic Albanian population from the province of Kosovo that was swallowed by those eager to punish Serbs in the early weeks of NATO's 1999 war. The U.S. establishment gave its full support to this Israeli invasion, with virtually unanimous Senate and House votes defending it. Two weeks into the bloodbath, only five members of the House voted against a resolution expressing "vigorous and unwavering commitment" to the "survival of the State of Israel as a Jewish and democratic state," as well as Israel's "right to act in self-defense to protect its citizens against Hamas's unceasing aggression, as enshrined in the United Nations Charter"; while on the Senate floor, Democratic Majority Leader Harry Reid noted that the Senate's resolution reaffirmed "Israel's inalienable right to defend [itself] against attacks from Gaza." At the swearing-in ceremony two weeks later for Secretary of State Hillary Clinton, President Barack Obama was no less emphatic: "America is committed to Israel's security," he said, and "will always support Israel's right to defend itself against legitimate threats."[175]

 There was much concern over Hamas's ability to attack Israel and to smuggle weapons into Gaza via tunnels and other means. But there was no one within the establishment prepared to argue that the Gaza Palestinians also possess a right to defend themselves or that other states bear a "'responsibility to protect' a civilian population being collectively punished by policies that amount to a Crime Against Humanity" (UN Special Rapporteur for the Palestinian territories Richard Falk[176]). Much less that Israel's open pipeline to U.S. weapons as well as its own world-class military-industrial sector poses an existential threat not only to the Palestinians but also to peace in the Middle East. That Israel had been provoking the Gaza Palestinians by holding their territory under near-total siege since June 2007, blocking off access to food, medicines, humanitarian assistance, travel, and much else, and had caused a major humanitarian crisis in Gaza, as stressed by numerous UN and independent observers, including the Vatican's Council for Justice and Peace, whose minister compared this besieged territory to a "big concentration camp," was of no interest to the U.S. establishment.[177] Nor was Israel's cruel and anti-civilian targeting and methods of warfare in its bombing and invasion, with undeniable use of white phosphorus weapons, all clearly designated war crimes by UN and other observers—though "turkey-shoot" was also properly used to describe this attack.[178] Unlike the Security Council, where Israel's offensive was as always shepherded by the permanent veto of the United States, the UN Human Rights Council in Geneva adopted a resolution "strongly condemn[ing] the ongoing Israeli military operation," calling for "international action to put an immediate end to the grave violations committed by the occupying Power," and for "international protection of the Palestinian people. . . ."[179] But among the major sectors of the U.S. establishment, the Palestinian response to the Israeli offensive and to massive prior violence is "terrorism" and the Palestinians resisting these conditions "militants"; Israeli violence, although killing many hundreds more civilians than the responsive "terrorism," and rooted in a system of long-term human rights abuses and dispossession perhaps without equal in the past forty years, is "self-defense" and "retaliation."[180]

The Gaza Palestinians remain *untermenschen* for the Israelis, for U.S. officials, for establishment pundits, and for leaders of the E.U. As victims of a U.S.-armed and protected client state, they are "unworthy" and not classifiable as the victims of "genocide" or "massacres." At a double session of the UN Security Council on January 14 devoted to the "protection of civilians in armed conflict," the Israeli attack on the Gaza Palestinians was mentioned by speakers throughout the day, as was the doctrine of the "responsibility to protect," adopted by the UN General Assembly in September 2005.[181] But the clear application of this doctrine to the Gaza Palestinians then under attack was mentioned by one speaker only, Egypt's UN ambassador Maged Abdelaziz, late in the afternoon session.[182] Similarly, the Global Center for the Responsibility to Protect at the City University of New York, which had issued a statement in August 2008 dismissing Russia's claim at the time to be protecting South Ossetia's population against Georgia's aggression, issued no such statement dismissing Israel's claim to be protecting its population

against Hamas and its rockets, much less did the Center invoke
the "responsibility to protect" on behalf of the Gaza
Palestinians.[183] A search of both newspapers and wire services for
the twenty-three days of Israel's offensive finds that in only
eleven different items was the "responsibility to protect" applied
to the Gaza Palestinians, and none of these was in a mainstream
publication. Not surprisingly, the doctrine was invoked in thirteen different items as applying to the Israelis instead; e.g.,
"Israel, as a UN Member State, has the right and responsibility to
protect its citizens from these terrorist attacks" (B'nai B'rith
International, News Release, January 12).[184]

When the UN's Fact Finding Mission on the Gaza Conflict,
headed by the South African jurist and avowed Zionist Richard
Goldstone, published its assessment of Operation Cast Lead in
September 2009,[185] the report was immediately ridiculed in Israel
and within forty-eight hours dismissed by the Obama administration as well, with UN Ambassador Susan Rice expressing "very
serious concerns about many of the recommendations in the
report."[186] The Goldstone Commission found that the Israeli
onslaught had been carried out against the "people of Gaza as a
whole," extending from the destruction of life and limb to the
"destruction of food supply installations, water sanitation systems, concrete factories and residential houses," and, in short, the
"economic capacity of the Gaza Strip"—and leaving "no doubt
that responsibility lies in the first place with those who designed,
planned, ordered and oversaw the operations."[187]

A UN Environmental Program assessment released at the
same time concluded that the "sustainability of the Gaza Strip is
now in serious doubt." Years of underinvestment in Gaza's water
treatment facilities (extraction, sanitation, and desalination), the
Israeli military's deliberate targeting of its sanitation and electrical
systems, an Israeli embargo that prevents the importation of spare
parts, and the Gaza's "overused" and "severely damaged" coastal
aquifer (the region's sole supply of fresh water which is now con-

taminated by waste and toxic chemicals, as well as by seepage from the Mediterranean Sea) mean that this strip of land some forty-one kilometers long and twelve kilometers wide at its maximum is no longer capable of supporting the Gaza Palestinians' needs. "Unless the trend is reversed now," the UNEP warned, "damage could take centuries to reverse."[188] The Israelis' deliberate destruction of Gaza's infrastructure (especially its water, sewage, and electrical systems), as well as their blockade of the equipment needed to make repairs, is reminiscent of the deliberate U.S. destruction of Iraq's infrastructure in 1990–1991 and the U.S. and U.K. sanctions to prevent Iraq's recovery from late 1990 into 2003. In both cases, the mass suffering and deaths caused by these policies are regarded as a "price" that is "worth it" to the policymakers. For its part, the "international community" evades any mention of a "responsibility to protect" large civilian populations under siege by Western powers.

Even though the Goldstone Commission devoted substantial sections to the conduct of the Gaza Palestinians, in particular their firing of rockets into southern Israel (extremely marginal actions relative to the scale of the IDF's attack on the Gaza Palestinians, with only one Israeli death for every one hundred Palestinian deaths), Goldstone, his Commission, and the UN Human Rights Council which sponsored the inquiry were savaged. The report "does not distinguish between the aggressor and the defender," went the Israeli line (President Shimon Peres), and "gives de facto legitimacy to terrorist initiatives and ignores the obligation and right of every country to defend itself."[189] Peres can say this without eliciting laughter because in the West Israel only responds to the violence of others, but never initiates it, and Israel's steady dispossession of the Palestinians is normalized—"ethnic cleansing" takes place only when dispossession is carried out by a target state such as Serbia. "Israel justly defended itself against terror," Israeli Prime Minister Benjamin Netanyahu said. "This biased and unjust report is a clear-cut test for all govern-

ments. Will you stand with Israel or will you stand with the terrorists?"[190] But in fact Netanyahu's own definition of terrorism
would include the Israeli attack on the Gaza Palestinians:
"Terrorism is the deliberate and systematic murder, maiming,
and menacing of the innocent to inspire fear for political ends."[191]
This is how Goldstone, and John Dugard and Richard Falk before
him, describe Israeli actions in Gaza. But Israel is free to kill and
ethnically cleanse *untermenschen*, given a remarkable system of
propaganda that overwhelms truth and morality.

Another line of attack on the Goldstone report stressed what
it could mean for Israel's Western allies "if the methodology and
conclusions of this infamous report were ever applied generally to
democracies seeking to combat terrorists who hid behind civilians—as in Afghanistan, Pakistan and Iraq," as Harvard's Alan
Dershowitz warned. The Israeli political scientist Gerald
Steinberg added that the "same terms could be applied to NATO
officials responsible for the deaths of civilians in strikes against
Taliban assets, such as oil trucks in Afghanistan. American troops
who used white phosphorous to protect against detection in the
battle of Fallujah in Iraq could be accused, like the Israelis targeted by Mr. Goldstone, of war crimes."[192]

In effect, these authors argue for Israel's exemption from the
rule of law on the ground that the United States is exempt! As the
United States enjoys impunity, no matter what it does to the
Afghan and Iraqi *untermenschen*, surely Israel should enjoy the
same impunity where the Palestinians are concerned.

But the fears expressed by Dershowitz and Steinberg about
Israeli vulnerability before the rule of law are unjustified: Israel
has been exempt from the rule of law from time immemorial and
remains exempt to this day. As a primary client of the United
States, Israel repeatedly violates the Fourth Geneva Convention
as an occupying power of the Palestinian Gaza Strip and the
Palestinian West Bank. For decades, Israel has illegally detained
thousands of Palestinians and used torture against them. It has

committed major aggressions against Lebanon and for a long
period maintained a terrorist army inside Lebanon. But throughout all of this, Israel has never once been subjected to international sanctions. Nor is there any reason to believe that something punitive will result from the Goldstone Commission. The
Goldstone Commission recommended that after six months'
time (roughly, by the spring of 2010), "in the absence of good
faith investigations that are independent and in conformity with
international standards," the Gaza attack should be referred to the
Prosecutor of the International Criminal Court for further investigation.[193] This will never happen. Indeed, several days before
Goldstone presented his report to the UN Human Rights
Council in Geneva, Susan Rice took issue with its "fundamental
problem": the Commission "was hatched with a bias inherent in
its mandate," namely, to investigate *both* Israeli and Palestinian
crimes, not just Palestinian. After Goldstone presented his findings, the U.S. representative, Michael Posner, rejected them as
"unbalanced" and "deeply flawed," and warned that Washington
would continue its fight against the Council's "double standards
and disproportionate focus on Israel." The U.S. rejected the
report and was joined in this by the E.U., both forcing the Council
to delay a vote on the report at least until March 2010, effectively
burying its recommendations.[194] The United States also
announced that it will block any effort on the part of the Security
Council to refer Israel to the ICC, and it is clear that no *ad hoc* tribunal will be established to investigate and prosecute Israel's
crimes. Israel will remain free to dispossess, to ethnically cleanse,
and to commit aggression. Israel enjoys client-state impunity.

As shown in Table 3, Israel's attack on Gaza was referred to
quite often as "genocide" (sixty times in twenty-three days)—
more times than any other massacre in our sample except
Srebrenica. But the Israeli attack was never once called "genocide" by any executive branch or high-ranking congressional
leader, mainstream pundit, or editorial. Of the major U.S. news-

papers, the *Christian Science Monitor* once cited a statement by Hezbollah that used the word ("The militant Shiite Hezbollah has led calls of condemnation in Lebanon, declaring the attack on Gaza an 'Israeli war crime and represents genocide,'" December 29, 2008), and the *New York Times* closed its report about the Israeli shelling of a UN school that killed forty Palestinians, mostly women and children, with a quote from Venezuela's Hugo Chávez ("Mr. Chávez . . . described Israel's actions in Gaza as 'genocide,'" January 7, 2009). But this was it: The rest were either smaller U.S. newspapers or foreign-based English language newspapers (though the *Washington Post* did run an op-ed by a Jewish academic in Jerusalem who stated that "Israelis are united today about our right to defend ourselves against Gaza's genocidally minded regime," January 4, 2009).

We believe that the reason "genocide" has been applied to the Gaza Palestinians so often by those who do use it is that the word does in fact fit Israeli plans and actions in Gaza and the West Bank so very well. Israeli leaders have often referred to Palestinians with racist derogation ("roaches," "grasshoppers," and "two-legged beasts"); some of them have spoken openly about their desire to transfer Palestinians out of the promised land or make their lives sufficiently miserable so as to move voluntarily; and Cast Lead was but one of many similar operations in which Palestinians are freely killed and their social fabric badly damaged. This is a *genocide-in-process*, moving slowly but relentlessly, and with the steady support of the Enlightened West. But we will certainly not see it called by its proper name by Samantha Power, David Rieff, Aryeh Neier, or the editors and pundits of the *New York Times*.

3. CROATIA'S OPERATION STORM

In the course of its struggle to break away from the Socialist Federal Republic of Yugoslavia, Croatia made a determined effort to crush and to ethnically cleanse the very large number of Serbs remaining in Croatian territory. They first did this to the Serb inhabitants of Western Slavonia via Operation Flash in May 1995. Later and far more extensively, in August 1995, Croatia launched Operation Storm against the Serbs living in the Krajina region, where Croatia shares a very long border with Bosnia and Herzegovina. These operations received critical U.S. support in terms of material aid and intelligence, the training of both Croat and Bosnian Muslim troops by corporate U.S. mercenaries such as MPRI (Military Professional Resources Inc.), and by diplomatic protection.[195] Coming less than one month after the Srebrenica massacre, Operation Storm drove some 250,000 ethnic Serbs out of the Krajina along both sides of the Croatia-Bosnia border, killing several thousand, including several hundred women and children. On the day in August when the Security Council took up the situations in both Bosnia and Croatia, U.S. Ambassador Madeleine Albright spoke in graphic terms about how "important" it was to "focus international attention on the plight of the refugee population from Srebrenica and Zepa," numbering some thirteen thousand by her reckoning, who the "Pale Serbs beat, raped and murdered." But she said nothing comparable about the twenty times larger cleansing of Serbs from the Krajina, using Srebrenica as a cover for this still ongoing operation carried out with blitzkrieg-like efficiency.[196]

This ethnic cleansing of 250,000 Serbs was the single largest event of its kind in the Balkan wars. On ICTY logic, the Croat leaders of Operation Storm could have been prosecuted for genocide. Consider the ICTY's reasoning in its *Judgment* for its first case related to Srebrenica, where it accepted that the "intent to eradicate a group within a limited geographical area such as the region of a country or even a municipality may be characterized as genocide."[197] Indeed, Operation Storm was nothing if not intended to kill or remove all Serbs from the Krajina, an area vastly larger than Srebrenica. In his testimony during the one Operation Storm–related case to be prosecuted at the ICTY, Peter Galbraith, the U.S. Ambassador to Croatia at the time, specifically recalled that "He [Franjo Tudjman] believed that . . . European states were much better off if they were ethnically homogeneous," and that Tudjman "saw because of their geography that the Krajina Serbs were a particular threat . . . located, after all, in such a way that they almost divided the northern part of Croatia from the coast." Galbraith also recalled a conversation with one of Tudjman's closest aides, who told him: "We cannot accept them to come back. They are a cancer in the stomach of Croatia."[198]

But as Operation Storm was both U.S.-sponsored and helped clear up Croatia's Serb problem, it was minimally newsworthy and has been treated neither as a massacre nor as genocide, as we can see in Table 3. In fact, although it was as clear a case of deliberate and massive ethnic cleansing as one could find, even the "ethnic cleansing" designation so prevalent in the coverage of these wars was denied by Peter Galbraith himself: "It is not ethnic cleansing," he said over BBC radio during Operation Storm. "Ethnic cleansing is a practice sponsored by the leadership in Belgrade carried out by the Bosnian Serbs and also by the Croatian Serbs of forcibly expelling the local population, whether it was Muslim or Croat, using terror tactics."[199] Actually, Galbraith's crude parsing of a military tactic according to its perpetrators and victims—"ethnic cleansing" *if* carried out by ethnic Serbs against Muslims or Croats, but *not if* carried out by their forces against ethnic Serbs—revealed a great deal about the U.S. and Western approach to the Balkan wars and many other theaters of conflict as well. The U.S. media in general used and continue to use the phrase pretty much in lockstep with Galbraith's usage here. Operation Storm was a Benign ethnic cleansing and bloodbath and is treated accordingly by the Free Press and the humanitarian intervention intellectuals.

4. DASHT-E-LEILI (AFGHANISTAN)

In November 2001, after the U.S.-allied Northern Alliance had captured thousands of Taliban fighters, several thousand of the prisoners were taken from jail, stuffed into some twenty-five containers, with about two hundred prisoners in each container, forty-five hundred prisoners in all, and driven to a final destination in the Dasht-e-Leili desert. A majority died *en route* of suffocation, and many were shot dead on arrival and buried in a huge gravesite bigger than any found in Bosnia. The estimates of numbers dead in this atrocity range from 961 to four thousand.[200]

Newsweek reported in "The Death Convoy of Afghanistan" that a confidential UN memo stated that while the facts of Dasht-e-Leili "are sufficient to justify a full-fledged investigation," the problem is "the political sensitivity of this case," and, as such, all action should be postponed "until a decision is made concerning the final goal of this exercise."[201] Translated from gobbledygook: As the United States was closely involved in these crimes, forget it. (In his 2002 documentary *Massacre at Mazar*, Irish filmmaker Jamie Doran provided compelling witness evidence that U.S. Army, Special Forces, and CIA personnel were on the scene, did not interfere with the operation, and at various points seemed in charge.)

The U.S.-based Physicians for Human Rights (PHR) said, "The examination of bodies and dignified burial of remains [from Dasht-e-Leili] will contribute to the truth and accountability process which is essential for future peace and stability in Afghanistan." But PHR is mistaken: This line of argument is only applicable in places like the former Yugoslavia in justifying the pursuit of villains—it is not applicable in places like Afghanistan and Indonesia where the possible villains are "our kind of guy" (a Clinton official on Indonesia's Suharto). While PHR, Amnesty International, and, to a lesser extent, Human Rights Watch gave some attention to Dasht-e-Leili, with PHR lobbying the U.S. government as early as 2002 to guard the integrity of the mass grave at Dasht-e-Leili for future investigation,[202] no protection was forthcoming. When PHR warned in December 2008 that "large sections of the Dasht-e-Leili mass grave in Northern Afghanistan have been dug up and removed," a spokesman for the U.S. commander of the International Security Assistance Force in Afghanistan dismissed calls to protect the grave, explaining that "protection of the site is not within the [ISAF's] mandate."[203] In short, as the United States was closely involved in these crimes, protection of the mass graves has not and will not happen in U.S.-controlled Afghanistan. But the "international community" will still be encouraged to protect and exhume mass graves in Bosnia, Iraq (i.e., provided they were filled by Saddam's regime), and Darfur.

When Jamie Doran's *Massacre at Mazar* was shown in preliminary form in Europe in June 2002, the European media gave it some attention, although brief, but the film was not mentioned once by the mainstream U.S. media. *Newsweek*'s substantial article on "The Death Convoy of Afghanistan" led to a tiny flurry of reports elsewhere in the media, after which it was quickly dropped. When the young British men known as the Tipton Three were released from U.S. custody in Guantánamo Bay in early March 2004, among their other revelations was their personal experience barely surviving the "death convoy." While this was reported in the British media, the *New York Times* failed to mention this feature of the disclosures. As we can see on Table 3, this gruesome massacre was never once described as a "massacre," let alone "genocide," in the newspapers. It was a Benign bloodbath, and on the borderline of the Constructive with such heavy U.S. involvement; hence neither newsworthy nor the basis of indignation and calls for justice.

After years of disinterest in this case, the *New York Times* returned to it in July 2009 with a front-page article and editorial.[204] The editors denounce as a "sordid legacy" of the Bush administration its "refusal to investigate charges" of these killings.

"There can be no justification for the horrors or for the willing-
ness of the United States and Afghanistan to look the other way,"
the *Times* editorialized. But the truth of the matter is that when
the Bush administration refused to "investigate charges" and
"looked the other way" back in 2001 and 2002, so did the *New
York Times*. The paper published no editorials or opinion
columns on the case, and only two news articles by foreign correspondent John Burns dealt with the Dasht-e-Leili massacre (the
word "massacre," incidentally, being one that Burns never applies
to this case), neither published until August 2002.[205] That was it
for the *Times* until July 2009. During this seven-year period there
were several opportunities to look more closely at the subject and
bring it to public attention, but the *Times* failed to do so. The
Bush administration wanted the U.S. media to look the other
way—and the *Times* obliged. So the "sordid legacy" of George
Bush is also a part of the sordid legacy of the *New York Times*.

But what caused the *Times* to change its focus in the summer
of 2009? The editors are open about it. As they note, "the administration is pressing Mr. Karzai not to return General Dostum
[the Afghan warlord in charge of the Dasht-e-Leili prisoners] to
power. Mr. Obama needs to order a full investigation into the
massacre. The site must be guarded and witnesses protected."[206]
Now, the editors acknowledge that back in 2001 Dostum "was on
the C.I.A. payroll and his militia worked closely with United
States Special Forces in the early days of the war." But seven years
earlier, in August 2002, John Burns reported instead that the Joint
Chiefs of Staff Vice-Chairman General Peter Pace had told a news
conference that an "internal review conducted by the United
States military had turned up no evidence that American troops
were in any way involved in what happened at Shibarghan
[*sic*]."[207] At that time, General Dostum was doing what the
Pentagon wanted him to do. But now the Pentagon and Obama
administration want Dostum out of the way, and the news fit to
print at the *Times* changes accordingly.

5. TURKEY'S KURDS VS. IRAQ'S KURDS

Over many years, both Turkey and Iraq have massively abused their Kurdish populations, which occupy land in the common border regions of northern Iraq, southeastern Turkey, north-eastern Syria, and northwestern Iran. Iraq's massacres, destruction of villages, and ethnic cleansing campaign against its Kurds under Saddam Hussein's rule achieved great notoriety, but only following Iraq's 1990 invasion of Kuwait and the first Gulf War in 1991. The largest body of indictments for which members of the former regime have been tried before the Iraqi Special Tribunal—and for which it sentenced Saddam to hang—pertain to this earlier campaign.

Beginning in the mid-1980s and continuing into this decade, successive regimes in Turkey have carried out their own systematic program to crush Kurdish nationalism, killing perhaps thirty thousand Kurds, destroying some thirty-five hundred villages, setting as many as three million refugees afoot, and for many years prohibiting expressions of "Kurdish" identity under a national law.[208] This murderous program was generously supported by successive U.S. administrations, reaching its peak in the mid-1990s under Bill Clinton.[209] Saddam Hussein was also vicious in dealing with his Kurds throughout the 1980s, with tens-of-thousands killed in the al-Anfal campaign. The most infamous incident in the al-Anfal campaign was the Halabja massacre, where Saddam's forces used chemical weapons, killing thousands. But that was back in March 1988, when Saddam was still a U.S. ally and prosecuting his war against the Islamic state of Iran. As the United States was among Saddam's suppliers of "weapons of mass destruction," critiques of the Halabja massacre were limited at the time, only to soar in the aftermath of Iraq's August 1990 invasion of Kuwait, the first Gulf War, the U.S.-UK invasion-occupation of 2003–2009, and the eventual show trials of Saddam and his associates. Table 3 shows that Halabja produced 122 newspaper items that mention "massacre'"and ten that mention "genocide." These numbers reflect the nefarious quality of the Iraqi leadership—at least after Saddam became "another Hitler" with his invasion of Kuwait in 1990.

An earlier study that compared the use of the word "genocide" to describe Turkey's treatment of its Kurds and Saddam's treatment of Iraq's Kurds in five major U.S. print media sources from 1990 to 1999 found that the term was used in Turkey's case in 14 different items, versus 132 for Iraq's. The print media in this sample devoted twenty-four front-page articles to stories that mentioned Saddam's "genocide," but only one front-page story mentioned Turkey's "genocide."[210] The same pattern holds true even if we greatly expand our print media universe and the time-horizon surveyed. Although attributions of "genocide" in relation to Turkey were common for the twenty-five-year period from 1984 to 2008, virtually all of these (99.8 percent) were made in relation to the Ottoman Empire's slaughter of the Armenian population from around 1915–1917 (i.e., in the distant past), with the minuscule remainder (0.2 percent) having been applied to Turkey's treatment of its Kurds in the contemporary period. Similarly, although attributions of "genocide" were made during this twenty-five-year period to show how different states treated their Kurds, virtually all of these (93.7 percent) focused on how Saddam treated Iraq's Kurds, again with the modest remainder (6.3%) left over to describe how Turkey treated its Kurds.[211] This contrast underscores not only a remarkably deep bias but also a consistent, even a rigid one over a very long period of time. The worthiness of Kurdish victims rises or falls in accord with the identity of their tormentors: An official enemy of the United States, like Saddam Hussein's regime from August 1990 on, produces worthy Kurdish victims; a key U.S. ally and member of the NATO bloc, like Turkey, does not.

6. INDONESIA AND EAST TIMOR—LIQUIÇÁ

When Indonesia invaded East Timor in December 1975, it did
this with U.S. approval and military and diplomatic aid. "Suharto
was given the green light [by the U.S.] to do what he did," C.
Philip Liechty, a former CIA operations officer at the U.S.
embassy in Jakarta, told John Pilger. As well, says Liechty, "without continued heavy U.S. logistical military support the
Indonesians might not have been able to pull it off."[212] But U.S.
assistance also reached into the UN Security Council. Given the
task of rendering the United Nations "utterly ineffective" in whatever measures it might take to reverse Indonesia's aggression,
U.S. Ambassador Daniel Patrick Moynihan bragged that he "carried it forward with no inconsiderable success."[213]

    It followed that the subsequent deaths of 200,000
Timorese—a larger percentage of the population than those who
died under Khmer Rouge rule in Cambodia—were treated gently
in the U.S. media. *New York Times* coverage of East Timor fell to
zero in 1977 and 1978, as U.S. military aid to Indonesia quadru-
pled under Jimmy Carter and Indonesian terror reached its pin-
nacle. Misleading apologetics for the Suharto dictatorship were
prevalent throughout this era of mass killing.[214] In the rare case
where the word "genocide" was mentioned in the *New York
Times*, reporter Henry Kamm dismissed it in 1981 as an oversim-
plification of the complex basis of the huge death toll: "accusations of 'genocide' rather than mass deaths from cruel warfare and
the starvation that accompanied it on this historically food-short
island" were the merest "hyperbole," Kamm insisted. He added
that as the "bulk of the testimony has come from highly partisan
members or supporters of [the Timorese resistance] Fretilin," the
world should treat such reports skeptically, in contrast to the
denials by Indonesian officials. East Timor simply "does not qualify for a busy world's attention," Kamm repeated several years
later (1987).[215] Kamm was right: The media of that "busy world"

paid minimal attention to East Timor under five consecutive U.S. presidential administrations (Gerald Ford through Bill Clinton), as Indonesia's twenty-four-year rampage was both an approved genocide and a Benign bloodbath.

Very much the same pattern was repeated in 1998–1999.[216] Following Suharto's replacement in May 1998, in the midst of a severe economic collapse in much of the region and mounting pressures at the United Nations to deal with the Timorese question once and for all, an agreement was reached in May 1999 permitting a referendum among the Timorese on whether to accept or reject their permanent integration with Indonesia. In an effort to make sure the referendum would not take place or that the Timorese would at least approve the outcome desired by Jakarta, the Indonesians launched yet another campaign of terror and killings, the violence dramatically increasing in the months before the UN agreement and culminating in the weeks after the vote on August 30. Although the Indonesian army began staging large troop withdrawals from East Timor as early as the summer of 1998, inviting Western reporters to witness the event, it was even then organizing paramilitary groups to carry out the terror campaign against pro-independence Timorese at its behest.[217] After the 1999 terror was well underway, Allan Nairn found the "chief-of-staff" of thirteen of these militias, who admitted that his groups had been given a "license to kill" by the Indonesian army.[218] Later, Nairn learned that after the April 6 massacre at the Catholic church in Liquiçá, where between sixty and two hundred civilians were slaughtered,[219] Admiral Dennis Blair, then the Commander in Chief of the U.S. Pacific Fleet (and in 2009 appointed Obama's Director of National Intelligence), was dispatched to Jakarta to meet with the Indonesian military leadership. But "at no point" did Blair tell Indonesia "to stop the militia operation," Nairn reported, based on a reading of U.S. documents. Instead, the Indonesian military took Blair's visit no doubt in the way Blair intended it—as a "green light to proceed with the militia operation."[220]

Less than three months before the Liquiçá massacre there had been the Račak massacre in Kosovo, which involved far fewer deaths (and, as shown below, was also mythical). As we can see on Table 3, Račak was referred to as a "massacre" in our newspaper universe three times more often than was Liquiçá, although the latter was quite real and with larger numbers killed. Noting the contradictions between the "high-minded rhetoric from NATO" about protecting human rights in Kosovo but not East Timor, Fretilin's Jose Ramos-Horta listed NATO's bombing war against Serbia, its demands for Serbian troop withdrawals from Kosovo (itself a province within Serbia), and its calls for the prosecution of Serbian officials by the ICTY—none of which were applied to the leadership of Indonesia's military forces, "many of whom have received training in NATO countries" and been the recipient of Western military largesse for decades.[221] But whereas the Račak massacre was serviceable to U.S. policy interests at the time, providing a convenient justification for NATO's coming war on Serbia, the Liquiçá massacre was not helpful: Liquiçá was a massacre by a valued client enjoying decades of U.S. support and approval, carried out while the "busy world" was focused on claims of "genocide" in Kosovo.

7. EL SALVADOR AND GUATEMALA

The United States supported regimes of terror for decades in Central America. Confining ourselves to El Salvador and Guatemala, we note that the UN Commission on the Truth for El Salvador was clear on the government's and government-supported paramilitaries' primary responsibility for the many thousands of civilian deaths and numerous massacres from 1980–1991.[222] A separate Truth Commission found the same to be true regarding Guatemala, and provided a countrywide map showing a reported 669 different massacre sites for 1962–1996. No fewer than 626 of

them were carried out during the "so-called scorched-earth operations [of the early 1980s], as planned by the State, [and resulting] in
the complete extermination of many Mayan communities."[223]

These Truth Commissions failed to stress the importance of
U.S. origination, support, and protection of the two regimes of
terror. Both the Salvadoran and the Guatemalan regimes received
financial support under U.S. congressional legislation that
claimed the aid to be "counter-terror," when in fact this was aid
directed to very serious perpetrators of state terrorism. In both
countries, "demonstration elections" were held under systems of
terror that made them a substantive farce, but gave the false
impression of a slackening of military control in "fledgling democracies," which with U.S. media cooperation helped make palat-
able U.S. support of these terror regimes.[224]

Among the many massacres in El Salvador, one of the most
vicious was carried out in December 1981 by the U.S.-trained
Atlacatl Battalion in the peasant village of El Mozote, where some
eight hundred to a thousand civilians, including several hundred
children, were slaughtered in cold blood. But its notoriety
stemmed not only from its magnitude, but in part because the
Wall Street Journal editors, furious at Raymond Bonner of the
New York Times for reporting this slaughter, denounced him and
labeled him a traitor, helping assure his rapid removal from this
beat.[225] We can see from Table 3 that while this episode has in fact
been called a "massacre" in 122 different items since 1982, it was
referred to as "genocide" only once.[226] The contrast in usage of
the "massacre" label between El Mozote and the two cases stemming from the wars in the former Yugoslavia at the Sarajevo mar-
ketplaces, Račak and especially Srebrenica, is dramatic.

Guatemala's short-lived democracy was terminated with the
U.S.-organized overthrow of the Arbenz government in 1954.
There followed a counterinsurgency and terror state that carried
out systematic warfare against any organized popular or dissident
groups, many only coming into existence to resist the brutal state-

terror. The successive military rulers could count on regular U.S. support in their anti-democratic and bloody campaigns. In 1980, Amnesty International published a study of Guatemala titled *A Government by Political Murder,* and Guatemala was also featured in another AI study called *Disappearances: A Case Study.* The 1999 report by the Truth Commission found that by far the greatest percentage of these state-organized massacres were carried out in a single department, El Quiche (45 percent), overwhelmingly against its indigenous Mayan population (83 percent). The Commission concluded that "many massacres and other human rights violations committed against these groups obeyed a higher, strategically planned policy, manifested in actions which had a logical and coherent sequence," adding that "agents of the State of Guatemala, within the framework of counterinsurgency operations carried out between 1981 and 1983, committed acts of genocide against groups of Mayan people. . . ."[227]

The exact numbers killed in these hundreds of massacres is unknown, but may run to 200,000 or more. Such large numbers, the focus on the Mayan population, and the evidence of high-level planning, makes this period of Guatemala's history a much better example of the Nuremberg (or ICTY-ICC) definitions of conspiracy, crimes against humanity, "joint criminal enterprise," and genocide than any incidents stemming form Bosnia's civil wars. But the perpetrator was a U.S. client state, fighting "Communism." Therefore, its massacres were Benign and its victims unworthy and downplayed by the media. Indeed, no "international" tribunal was formed to investigate and try the perpetrators—only a Commission for Historical Clarification. Although many more were killed in this war on the Mayan Indians than in Bosnia in the 1990s, "Guatemala" does not show up in the index of Samantha Power's book, whose subtitle is "America and the Age of Genocide."

Table 3 includes Guatemala's March 1982 massacre at Rio Negro, where an estimated 444 Mayans were slaughtered. A Rio

Negro "massacre" turns up in twenty-one different items in our newspaper universe, but never a Rio Negro "genocide," and never Rio Negro as one link in a lengthy chain of massacres that, taken as a whole, more appropriately would be called "genocide." Note that though the word "genocide" is applied to Bosnia 481 times in Table 1 and to Srebrenica 442 times in Table 3, the latter also shows that our newspaper universe used it only once for El Mozote and never for Rio Negro. This parallels news coverage and reflects deep political bias. It should also be noted that the *New York Times* never once cited the two devastating Amnesty studies of Guatemala published in 1980 and 1981 and that a separate analysis showed that twenty-three murdered Guatemala religious figures, including one U.S. citizen, got less than one-tenth the coverage of the single murder of the Polish priest Jerzy Popieluszko.[228] Here, as before, the difference is that the twenty-three were killed by a client-perpetrator, making their deaths unworthy. In contrast, Popieluszko was killed by an enemy-perpetrator, the then-Communist state of Poland, a Nefarious case and a worthy victim, reported often and with great indignation and with an unremitting search for responsibility at the top.

"immediate and unimpeded access" to Kosovo and planned to travel there within forty-eight hours. [229] Suddenly, a heavily fortified village that almost no one had heard of before, half an hour's drive south from the capital city, Pristina, was headline news in every major Western newspaper.

The "Račak massacre" of January 15, 1999 was extremely convenient for Clinton administration officials and NATO. The incident served as a "turning point" that led NATO to "authorize air strikes against targets on [Federal Republic of Yugoslavia] territory" and to NATO's ultimatum to the Serb leadership in Belgrade to engage in one last round of talks at Rambouillet—itself one of the great make-believe pieces of stagecraft in recent memory, designed to ensure that NATO could carry out its bombing war in time for its Fiftieth Anniversary Summit in Washington in April. When Madeleine Albright was first informed about the Račak incident, she enthused that "Spring has come early to Kosovo."[230] News of the deaths of some forty Kosovo Albanians (one woman and thirty-nine men) was delivered directly to her by William Walker, a veteran U.S. administrator of Reagan-era wars in Central America, now assigned to the Kosovo Verification Mission, an Organization for Security and Cooperation in Europe (OSCE) mission in name only and in fact a U.S. mission to prepare for war.[231] Walker rushed to Račak on the morning of January 16, instantly proclaimed it a "massacre," and demanded accountability before the ICTY. That this was the same career U.S. apparatchik who, when serving as his government's ambassador to El Salvador in 1989, performed spectacular apologetics in defense of the Salvadoran army's massacre of six Jesuit priests, their housekeeper, and her daughter in November of that year was missed by virtually everybody.[232] "Management control problems exist in a situation like this," Walker explained when in El Salvador. "And it's not a management control problem that would lend itself to a Harvard Business School analysis. I mean, this is war." No deliberately executed bloodbath in El

Salvador, according to the ambassador, just heat-of-battle excesses; and no "war" in Kosovo, just a cold-blooded massacre. As the *Los Angeles Times* later observed, this self-presentation as a "crusader for human rights represents quite a change for Walker."[233] But he got away with it—this *Los Angeles Times* observation was virtually unique.

We do not believe there was any massacre at all at Račak.[234] In attacking this and other local Kosovo Liberation Army (KLA) strongholds (Belince, Malopoljce, Petrovo) on January 15, the Serb forces were accompanied not only by invited OSCE observers but also by an AP camera crew that filmed events throughout the action. Multiple firefights took place between the Serbs and KLA fighters in several locations, mostly outside the towns in the surrounding woods. Serb forces withdrew from the area long before sunset. Later that same day, the French reporter Christophe Chatelet visited Račak and met with OSCE observers, none of whom reported any incident resembling a massacre. But the next morning, after the return of the KLA to Račak during the night, twenty-two dead bodies were discovered in a gully outside the village and at least eighteen more at different sites inside the village. Why the Serbs had not removed or buried any of these bodies while present as a fighting force the previous day, and why the OSCE and AP camera crew had not reported such facts, has never been clarified—and OSCE personnel have never been allowed to speak publicly about it.

William Walker, arriving quickly to the scene on January 16, failed to preserve its integrity for forensic study and potentially important details were forever compromised; Walker also blocked forensic experts from examining the site and the bodies until January 22.[235] But the body-strewn gully did form the back-drop for Walker's famous denunciation that day: "From what I personally saw, I do not hesitate to describe the event as a massacre, obviously a crime very much against humanity. Nor do I hesitate to accuse the government security forces of responsibility."[236] Summing up the work of the Walker-led mission in Kosovo, KLA adviser Marc Weller argues that the "accidental [sic] discovery of the Račak massacre . . . made it difficult for NATO to legitimize its inaction."[237] For the "humanitarian" intervention regime a critical *casus belli* had been established.

The EU Forensic Team that began its work at University of Pristina on January 22 came to the site late, and its leader, Helena Ranta, was pressed by Walker and her government (Finland) to declare Račak a massacre of civilians and crime against humanity. This she eventually did, although contradictorily, relying on hearsay evidence from Walker and admitting that the EU Team never investigated the alleged crime scene and was unable to ascertain the chain of custody of the bodies between the time of death and the date when the autopsies began. Moreover, Ranta has been backtracking ever since her early claims, complaining about the political pressures under which she operated. A 2008 biography of Ranta published in Finland even quotes her saying that Walker "wanted me to say the Serbs were behind [the Račak massacre] so the war could begin."[238]

All of this points up the extent to which the "Račak massacre" was above all a *political artifact*, serving, as Ranta suggests, a war-justification role, with the supposed research that went into its codification requiring heavy discounting. In addition to the testimony of Chatelet and the circumstances of the Serb action of January 15, there is also forensic evidence that the bodies recovered on January 16 were combatants, not simply civilians. Gunpowder residue was found on the hands of thirty-seven of the forty bodies autopsied at Pristina University's Department of Forensic Medicine, according to the Serb forensic pathologist Dusan Dunjic, who worked with the EU Team; the "traces of gunpowder explosion indicated that directly before death, these people had handled firearms," he has written.[239]

Also of importance is a 2001 reassessment of the EU Team's findings.[240] Although the *cause* of death in all forty cases was gunshot wounds, the number of wounds varied widely across the forty bodies. Six bodies had only one gunshot wound, which of course proved fatal; but fifteen bodies had between two and five wounds, fourteen bodies between six and ten, and five bodies between eleven and twenty.[241] Yet, on the "massacre" model, in which between twenty-two and forty Kosovo Albanian civilians were rounded up by Serb forces and executed in cold blood, it is highly unlikely that six persons would have been executed by a single shot, while another thirty-four persons would have received between two and twenty bullet wounds. On the contrary, this variation in observable wounds suggests something else: Deaths occurring under a series of different circumstances (or different "manners of death," in the terminology used by these experts[242]) in different locations and at different times. What is more, in only eleven cases was a "considerable uniformity consistent with sustained firing . . . detected" in the forty bodies autopsied (or was "sustained firing . . . probable," as they put it elsewhere); otherwise, "Bullet path directions were mostly variable."[243] Taken in whole, this suggests that the killings in and around Račak as well as the other three villages where Serb forces carried out their offensive on January 15 were mainly, if not exclusively, battle deaths rather than executions. [244]

But Bill Clinton, Madeleine Albright, the ICTY, Louise Arbour, NATO, and the mainstream media all took their cues from Walker's first performance at the scene, and agreed unhesitatingly that Račak was a cold-blooded massacre of at least forty Kosovo Albanian civilians, thus establishing once again the ruthlessness and villainy of the Serbs. Bill Clinton repeatedly lied about Račak, even claiming in one nationally televised news conference just five days before the start of the war that "innocent men, women, and children [were] taken from their homes to a gully, forced to kneel in the dirt, sprayed with gunfire, not because of anything they had done, but because of who they were."[245] As we noted, Albright was positively delighted with William Walker's news about a "massacre." Louise Arbour quickly declared the "Račak massacre" a crime based solely on Walker's news about it. The EU's German president persuaded Helena Ranta to hold her news conference on March 17, where, under great pressure, she delivered a biased "personal" interpretation of the EU Forensic Team's work—March 17 turning out to be the very last day of the Rambouillet talks, thus helping to cancel out Belgrade's efforts to stave-off NATO's imminent war. Indeed, so important was the "Račak massacre" to NATO's march to war, this single incident on January 15, 1999, comprises the only charge in the ICTY's May 1999 indictment of Slobodan Milosevic for crimes that he allegedly committed in Kosovo that occurred *prior* to the start of NATO's bombing war.[246]

Media collaboration in turning the "Račak massacre" into a *casus belli* was exemplary. Most notable was the media's almost uniform failure to mention the circumstances of the Serb offensive: The KLA's killing of Serb police officers the weekend before; the invited presence of OSCE monitors, the AP camera crew, and a French journalist—or the incompetence of the Serb forces that left dead bodies strewn across the ground (and which nobody spotted, until the overnight return of the KLA to the village); or William Walker's background as an administrator of his government's foreign wars; or Bill Clinton's lie about Serb targeting of ethnic Albanian women and children "because of who they were"; or the pressures put on the EU Forensic Team and Helena Ranta; or the convenience of the "Račak massacre" for U.S. and NATO policy at the time. In short, a "massacre" served well the U.S. and NATO plans to launch a bombing war on the Federal Republic of Yugoslavia, already in the works for several months; and the media helped these powers to fashion the political artifact needed to make it real.

As can be seen in Table 3 the word "massacre" was used 312 times by the newspapers in discussing Račak, nearly three times more often than El Mozote, which involved between eighteen and twenty-two times as many deaths—real killings of civilians, not a mythical bloodbath based on atrocities management, and in the El Mozote case people for whom justice will never be obtained. If Račak is a mythical atrocity, as we believe, then the war that it helped sell to the world was based on a lie, and any notion that this war was in the pursuit of justice is called into question by this fact alone.

Concluding Note

During the past several decades, the word "genocide" has increased in frequency of use and recklessness of application,[247] so much so that the crime of the twentieth century for which the word originally was coined often appears debased. Unchanged, however, is the huge political bias in its usage, and it remains as true today as it was in 1973 or 1988 that "We can even read who are the U.S. friends and enemies from the media's use of the word." [248]

When we ourselves commit mass-atrocity crimes, the atrocities are *Constructive*, our victims are *unworthy* of our attention and indignation, and never suffer "genocide" at our hands—like the Iraqi *untermenschen* who have died in such grotesque numbers over the past two decades. But when the perpetrator of mass-atrocity crimes is our enemy or a state targeted by us for destabilization and attack, the converse is true. Then the atrocities are *Nefarious* and their victims *worthy* of our focus, sympathy, public displays of solidarity, and calls for inquiry and punishment. Nefarious atrocities even have their own proper names reserved for them, typically associated with the places where the events occur. We can all rattle off the most notorious: Cambodia (but only under the Khmer Rouge, not in the prior years of mass killing by the United States and its allies), Iraq (but only when attributable to Saddam Hussein, not the United States), and so on—Halabja, Bosnia, Srebrenica, Rwanda, Kosovo, Račak, Darfur. Indeed, receiving such a baptism is perhaps the hallmark of the Nefarious bloodbath.

Both the media and "genocide"-oriented intellectuals, and even leading NGOs, follow the official line on bloodbaths and genocide; and given the global power of the United States, so do E.U. and UN officials. The media and intellectuals "follow the flag," and the politics of genocide and massacre require the inflation of Nefarious bloodbaths, while ignoring or underplaying those that are Constructive or Benign. As we have shown, they will all, including the NGOs as well as UN officials, feature the Nefarious case of Darfur[249] and earlier Bosnia, Rwanda, and Kosovo, but not the Constructive and Benign bloodbaths in Central America, Iraq, the Democratic Republic of Congo, Afghanistan, and Palestine.

When the International Criminal Court's chief prosecutor Luis Moreno-Ocampo petitioned the Court in July 2008 to issue an arrest warrant for President Omar Hassan Ahmad al-Bashir of Sudan "in relation to 10 counts of genocide, crimes against humanity and war crimes" in the Darfur states of the western Sudan since 2003, this was the first case in which a head of state had received such honors from the ICC. (Just as Slobodan Milosevic in 1999 had become the first head of state ever to be indicted by an international tribunal while in office.) Moreno-Ocampo summed up the reason for this action, saying "[al-Bashir's] motives were largely political. His alibi was 'counterinsurgency'. His intent was genocide."[250]

And when in March 2009, the ICC eventually issued a warrant for the arrest of al-Bashir—to the resounding applause of the Western establishment[251]—on counts of crimes against humanity and war crimes (with genocide having been dropped, though Moreno-Ocampo later petitioned the Court to recon-

sider this count as well[252]), foremost among the Court's reasons
for affirming its jurisdiction "in the territory of a State not a party
to the [Rome] Statute" was one that it described in frankly political terms: "one of the core goals of the Statute," the Court
emphasized, "is to put an end to impunity for the perpetrators of
the most serious crimes of concern to the international community as a whole, which 'must not go unpunished'."[253] Whatever
the case's merits, issuing an arrest warrant for the President of
Sudan contributes to a higher good—or so the Court maintains—in that it advances a long-term goal of international justice: That the law not only applies to *all persons equally*, but can
be *seen* to apply to all persons equally or "without any distinction
based on official capacity."[254] Such was the ICC's explicit reasoning. The indictments against al-Bashir prove to the world that *no
man is above the law.*

The ICC judges' arrest warrant for the President of the Sudan
maintains this line, apparently without embarrassment, in face of
the fact that, through mid-2009, all fourteen of the ICC's
indictees were black Africans, while effectively immunizing two
other black African presidents (Uganda's Yoweri Museveni and
Rwanda's Paul Kagame) who are major killers, but also happen to
be major clients of the United States. No members of the Western
political establishment seem to find the ICC's selectivity a problem. Nor do the "human rights" and "international justice"
NGOs, which applaud every indictment the ICC issues.

Indeed, *ending impunity* and bringing about *accountability for
the mass slaughter of civilians,* implicitly without any distinction
relating to race and power, have been the promises of the ICC
from its very inception. When the negotiations that led to the
Rome Statute were completed in July 1998, then-Secretary-
General Kofi Annan flew to the Eternal City to attend the
Conference's closing ceremony. "Until now, when powerful men
committed crimes against humanity, they knew that as long as
they remained powerful, no earthly court could judge them,"

Annan said. But with the new ICC, all this will change. No longer will "[v]erdicts intended to uphold the rights of the weak and help-less . . . be impugned as 'victor's justice,'" he said, "because others have proved more powerful, and so are able to sit in judgment over them." No longer will courts set up on an *ad hoc* basis, "like the tri-bunals in The Hague and in Arusha, to deal with crimes commit-ted in specific conflicts or by specific regimes" be similarly impugned, as if the "same crimes, committed by different people, or at different times and places, will go unpunished. Now at last . . . we shall have a permanent court to judge the most serious crimes of concern to the international community as a whole: genocide, crimes against humanity and war crimes."[255]

But what Annan promised, the Rome Statute had already taken away. It is true that Article 5.1 lists the "crime of aggression" among the four "most serious crimes of concern to the interna-tional community as a whole" over which the ICC is to exercise jurisdiction (the other three being genocide, crimes against humanity, and war crimes). However, Article 5.2 adds that "The Court shall exercise jurisdiction over the crime of aggression [if and only if] a provision is adopted . . . defining the crime and set-ting out the conditions under which the Court shall exercise juris-diction with respect to this crime."[256] No definition has been forthcoming, despite the great and possibly increasing impor-tance of the crime in question, and despite the existence of a Special Working Group at the ICC since 2002 with the task of amending the Rome Statute accordingly.[257] Yet, even then, an amendment such as this "would have to be ratified by seven-eighths of the state parties to take effect," as York University's Michael Mandel points out, and "*it would only take effect against state parties who accepted it. . . .* In other words, no jurisdiction over the supreme crime until almost everybody agrees, and then an exemption for any signatory who wants it."[258] Clearly, this is no way to end the culture of impunity. In fact, it is the negation of the ancient maxim that *justice is blind.*

And while the ICC ensures impunity for those states which have proven the most powerful, it also fulfills what Mandel calls the "American desire for a permanent *ad hoc* court"—a kind of permanent ICTY and ICTR to deal with specific conflicts and specific regimes, "'a standing tribunal . . . that [can] be activated immediately' by the Security Council on a case-by-case basis,"[259] exactly as the Council did in adopting Resolution 1593 in March 2005, when, arguing that the Darfur crisis inside the western Sudan "continues to constitute a threat to international peace and security," the Council referred the case to the Prosecutor at the ICC.[260]Surely the al-Bashir case is a harbinger of how the Global South can expect both the ICC and R2P to be implemented going forward: A permanent *ad hoc* R2P to accompany the permanent *ad hoc* ICC.

We can only speculate what might come of comparable inquiries into the whole spectrum of U.S., NATO, and Israeli wars and occupations throughout the postwar era were these theaters of atrocity crimes referred to independent investigations as aggressive as the ICC Prosecutor's inquiry into the Sudan or those of the forensic teams that exhume and identify the remains of the dead from Bosnia and Herzegovina's civil wars and Saddam Hussein's rule in Iraq—or that of the International Military Tribunal for Germany at Nuremberg.

Yet, in dramatic contrast to these inquiries, the same Prosecutor at the ICC in February 2006 declined to initiate so much as an investigation into crimes committed in Iraq during the U.S. war and occupation, despite having received "over 240 communications" asking him to do so, including requests from Amnesty International and Human Rights Watch.

In the letter explaining his decision, Moreno-Ocampo gave multiple reasons why his office would not proceed with an investigation. Neither Iraq nor the United States have acceded to the ICC's jurisdiction, he argued, correctly;[261] the ICC remains as yet incapable of deciding "whether the *decision to engage* in armed conflict was legal" (for reasons discussed above, the crime of aggression does not yet fall under the ICC's jurisdiction); his office was "provided no reasonable indicia that [U.S.] forces had 'intent to destroy, in whole or in part, a national, ethnical, racial or religious group as such', as required in the definition of genocide"; and similar legal evasions.

But most remarkable of all, under crimes of war, the "targeting of civilians," "excessive attacks," "willful killings," and "inhuman treatment of civilians," the only category for which Moreno-Ocampo was willing to entertain the evidence shared with his office by the more than 240 interested parties, he still discovered a reason *not* to proceed: The Iraqi theater of atrocities, it appears, fails to meet the ICC's general "threshold of gravity" requirement. In Moreno-Ocampo's exact words, the killing and destruction in Iraq are:

> of a different order than the number of victims found in other situations under investigation or analysis by the Office. It is worth bearing in mind that the [Office of the Prosecutor] is currently investigating three situations involving long-running conflicts in Northern Uganda, the Democratic Republic of Congo and Darfur. Each of the three situations under investigation involves thousands of wilful killings as well as intentional and large-scale sexual violence and abductions. Collectively, they have resulted in the displacement of more than 5 million people. Other situations under analysis also feature hundreds or thousands of such crimes. Taking into account all the considerations, the situation did not appear to meet the required threshold of the Statute.[262]

As we have shown, the hundreds of thousands of Iraqi victims of the long-running "sanctions of mass destruction" era were "willfully" killed by a policy whose consequences were both understood and desired by the U.S. and British states enforcing it and even publicly claimed to be "worth it" by their perpetrators.

The one million (or more) "excess" Iraqi deaths from 2003 through 2009 have flowed directly from the "supreme international crime" committed by Iraq's U.S. and British invaders, as did the displacement of the Iraqi population on a scale comparable to the five million cited by Moreno–Ocampo as the "collective" number in three different theaters in Africa and far greater than the numbers displaced in Darfur alone.

It is also striking that the Office of the Prosecutor at the ICTY invoked a similar threshold-of-gravity objection, after it had been pressed to examine the U.S.-led NATO-bloc's 1999 bombing war against Serbia. In this case, Carla Del Ponte refused to open a formal investigation of possible NATO crimes, on the grounds that the total of 495 Serbs documented by her office to have been killed by NATO comprised an insufficiently large number—"there is simply no evidence of the *necessary crime base* for charges of genocide or crimes against humanity."[263] Yet one year earlier, her predecessor, Louise Arbour, had decided that 344 dead Kosovo Albanians crossed the threshold of gravity and comprised a sufficient crime-base to request the indictment of Yugoslav President Slobodan Milosevic for various crimes, which the ICTY promptly granted, even though only forty-five of these deaths were reported to have occurred prior to the start of NATO's war.[264] NATO's PR spokesman Jamie Shea explained the basis of the ICTY's choices in implementing its statute: "[W]ithout NATO countries there would be no International Court of Justice, nor would there be any International Criminal Tribunal for the former Yugoslavia because NATO countries are in the forefront of those who have established these two tribunals, who fund these tribunals and who support on a daily basis their activities. We are the upholders, not the violators, of international law."[265]

The ICTY indicted Milosevic for the killing of 344 Kosovo Albanians during a period of active warfare, and Serb killings at Srebrenica and Račak released enormous passions in the West, as well as serial indictments and prosecutions of key Serb figures. Yet, a September 1994 memorandum to the U.S. Secretary of State that Paul Kagame's RPF was killing "10,000 or more Hutu civilians *per month*" in Rwanda was suppressed by the Clinton administration, the UN, and the media, and Kagame was transformed into Africa's "Abraham Lincoln" (Philip Gourevitch). Indeed, Kagame and his RPF were quietly supported by the Free World as they greatly extended their conquest of territory and massacres into the Democratic Republic of Congo. As we have pointed out, Kagame was trained at Fort Leavenworth and enjoyed continuous U.S. support while he planned and executed the violent regime change in Rwanda. Kagame outshines Idi Amin as a killer,[266] but his impunity follows in the wake of this pattern of service and support.

In this and many other ways the global culture of impunity shows itself, as the United States and its allies get free passes on their "supreme international crimes," as well as any and all of the "accumulated evil" that issues from them. Likewise, when the Federal Republic of Yugoslavia asked the International Court of Justice to issue an injunction against ten member-states of the NATO bloc then bombing it in the spring of 1999, the United States responded in court that it had "not consented to the Court's jurisdiction in this case, and absent such consent, the Court has no jurisdiction to proceed."[267] As early as June 2, 1999, with *Yugoslavia still under attack by NATO*, the ICJ ruled that it "manifestly lacks jurisdiction" to entertain Yugoslavia's complaint naming the United States, and lacked the right to enjoin the aggressors from continuing with their attack. The ICJ "cannot decide a dispute between States without the consent of those States to its jurisdiction," twelve of fifteen judges agreed. Since the "United States observes that it 'has not consented to jurisdiction . . . and will not do so,'" the ICJ was left with no alternative: "in the absence of consent by the United States, . . . the Court cannot exercise jurisdiction. . . . "[268]

Flatly contradicting the rhetoric used by the ICC against the President of the Sudan, this much-heralded advance in universal jurisdiction, the first warrant of arrest ever issued for a sitting Head of State by the ICC,[269] the ICC struck at yet another black African whose killings ran afoul of the Great White-Northern Powers, but it stopped dead-in-its-tracks at the borders of NATO and its allies. Not only do their UN Charter-violating acts of aggression and mass-atrocity crimes go unpunished, but their notable persons, acting in their official capacities, remain as much beyond the reach of international law as ever. In this first decade of the twenty-first century, the United States, its allies, and its clients—but not its enemies in Sub-Saharan Africa and elsewhere—continue to benefit from the same global culture of impunity which the Great Unequals have always enjoyed, an impunity that is rooted neither in their goodness nor their justice but in their vastly superior economic and political power and nothing more.

The inability of any sector of the U.S. establishment to recognize fully that the human and material destruction in Southeast Asia and the Middle East are the consequence, not of accident, much less error, but of deliberate policies that produced this result, ranks among the greatest intellectual and moral failures in U.S. history. If the phrase *genocide denial* has any validity, we find it here, in the standard practice of the richest and most well-educated classes in the world.

Thus, the human capacity to ignore or to decry mass atrocities, depending on whether we commit them or our enemies commit them, is as observable today as at any other time. In 2003, a Pulitzer Prize in the nonfiction category was awarded to a tract whose author has honed the drawing of this distinction to a very high art;[270] and, throughout this decade, "humanitarian" war intellectuals have shifted quietly from the cause of the Bosniaks, Tutsi, and Kosovars to the cause of the Darfurians—or that of the Lebanese, the Tibetans, the Burmese, Iranian women and students (and the like). It is notorious how little attention is paid by the New Humanitarians to why those peoples were suddenly elevated to worthy-victim status, both before and after their usefulness on the geopolitical stage has come and gone.

Just as the guardians of "international justice" have yet to find a single crime committed by a Great White-Northern Power against people of color that crosses their *threshold of gravity*, so too all of the fine talk about the "responsibility to protect" and the "end of impunity" has never once been extended to the victims of these same powers, no matter how egregious the crimes. The Western establishment rushed to proclaim "genocide" in Bosnia-Herzegovina, Rwanda, Kosovo, and Darfur, and also agitated for tribunals to hold the alleged perpetrators accountable. In contrast, its silence over the crimes committed by its own regimes against the peoples of Southeast Asia, Central America, the Middle East, and Sub-Saharan Africa is deafening. *This* is the "politics of genocide."

Notes

1. No letters appeared in reaction. However, four months later (Oct. 8, 2009), the editors published a "clarification," which reads as follows: "In his review of Edmund S. Morgan's essay collection *American Heroes: Profiles of Men and Women Who Shaped Early America* [NYR, June 11] Russell Baker, drawing on the estimates mentioned in Morgans' 1958 essay 'The Unyielding Indian,' wrote that in North America at the time of Columbus, there may have been scarcely more than a million inhabitants. However, archaeological evidence and demographic research in recent decades suggest that the number was much larger, with estimates ranging up to 18 million."

   The "clarification" is perhaps even worse than the original. Baker was not referring to North America ("from the tropical jungle . . ."). Over thirty years ago it was well-known that in North America (as defined in NAFTA, including Mexico) the numbers were in the tens of millions, far more beyond; and that even in the U.S. and Canada the numbers were about ten million or more. It was also known, even well before, that the "sparsely populated . . . unspoiled world" included advanced civilizations (in the U.S. and Canada too). This remarkable episode remains "genocide denial with a vengeance," underscored by the "clarification."

2. *Memorandum by the Director of the Policy Planning Staff (Kennan) to the Secretary of State and the Under Secretary of State (Lovett)*, February 24, 1948, in *Foreign Relations of the United States*, 1948, Vol. 1, 524, http://images.library.wisc.edu/FRUS/EFacs/1948v01p2/reference/frus.frus1948v01p2.i0007.pdf.

3. See, e.g., Gabriel Kolko, *The Politics of War: The World and United States Foreign Policy, 1943–1945* (New York: Pantheon Books, 1990); and Joyce Kolko and Gabriel Kolko, *The Limits of Power: The World and United States Foreign Policy, 1945–1954* (New York: Harper & Row, 1972). On the U.S. military-industrial complex, see John Bellamy Foster, Hannah Holleman, and Robert W. McChesney, "The U.S. Imperial Triangle and Military Spending," *Monthly Review* 60, October, 2008, http://monthlyreview. org/081001foster-holleman-mcchesney.php. On the U.S. "empire of bases," see Chalmers Johnson, *Nemesis: The Last Days of the American Republic* (New York: Metropolitan Books, 2006); and Catherine Lutz, ed., *The Bases of Empire: The Global Struggle against U.S. Military Posts* (New York: Pluto Press, 2009).

4. *United States Objectives and Courses of Action with Respect to Latin America* (NSC 5432/1), September 3, 1954, in *Foreign Relations of the United States, 1952–1954*, Vol. IV, 81, http://images.library .wisc.edu/FRUS/EFacs2/1952-54v04/reference/frus.frus195254 v04.i0009.pdf.

5. See Noam Chomsky and Edward S. Herman, *The Washington Connection and Third World Fascism* (Boston: South End Press, 1979); and Edward S. Herman, *The Real Terror Network: Bloodbaths in Fact and Propaganda* (Boston: South End Press, 1982).

6. See the webpage maintained by William Blum, "United States waging war/military action, either directly or in conjunction with a proxy army" (last accessed in September 2009), http://killinghope.org/ bblum6/us-action.html.

7. See, e.g., Noam Chomsky, *On Power and Ideology: The Managua Lectures* (Boston: South End Press, 1987), esp. chap. 1, "The Overall Framework of Order," 5–26; Noam Chomsky, *Deterring Democracy* (New York: Hill and Wang, 1992), esp. the introduction and chap. 1, "Cold War: Fact and Fancy," 1–68.

8. Noam Chomsky and Edward S. Herman, *Counter-Revolutionary Violence: Bloodbaths in Fact and Propaganda* (Andover, MA: Warner Modular Publications, Inc., 1973), http://web.archive.org/web/ 20050313044927/ http://mass-multi-media.com/CRV.

9. *Ibid.,* 7.

10. See H. Bruce Franklin, *M.I.A. or Mythmaking In America* (New York: Lawrence Hill Books, 1992).

11. Chomsky and Herman, *The Washington Connection and Third World Fascism.* For its treatment of Warner CEO William Sarnoff's suppression of the original 1973 edition of CRV, "an authentic instance of private censorship of ideas per se," see xiv–xvii.

12. Samantha Power, "A Problem from Hell": America and the Age of Genocide (New York: Basic Books, 2002), 146–147; 94–95.

13. Roy Gutman, David Rieff, and Anthony Dworkin, eds., Crimes of War 2.0: What the Public Should Know (New York: W.W. Norton, 2007); Sydney Schanberg, "Cambodia," 78–79. Also see the Website of the Crimes of War Project, http://www.crimesofwar.org.

14. Aryeh Neier, War Crimes: Brutality, Genocide, Terror, and the Struggle for Justice (New York: Times Books, 1998), 93–95.

15. Robertson's use of the word "mistake" is misleading as Diem was literally imported from the United States and imposed on the South Vietnamese by U.S. power, and the U.S. actively supported his terroristic and undemocratic rule until 1963. See George McT. Kahin, Intervention (New York: Alfred Knopf, 1986), 78ff.

16. Geoffrey Robertson, Crimes Against Humanity: The Struggle for Global Justice (New York: The New Press, 2000), 41–42. Here we add that Robertson has defended ("might have been justifiable") the dropping of atomic bombs on Hiroshima and Nagasaki, under the concept of "military necessity, by bringing the war to a speedier end with less overall loss of life than would otherwise have been the case" (187). And in his penultimate chapter, "The Guernica Paradox," Robertson coined the phrase "Bombing for Humanity"—a phrase that will warm the heart of every serially aggressive power (401–436).

17. Christiane Amanpour, Scream Bloody Murder, CNN, December 4, 2008.

18. Madeleine K. Albright and William S. Cohen, Preventing Genocide: A Blueprint for U.S. Policymakers (Washington D.C.: United States Holocaust Memorial Museum, 2008), http://www.usip.org/genocide_taskforce/ report.html. This report does mention Indonesia in passing, but only with respect to USAID "mediation efforts in places such as Aceh" (40) and by way of explaining the nature of Washington's interest in stopping Jakarta's rampage in East Timor in 1999 (56, 70). But it never mentions Indonesia as the perpetrator of the mass killings of the 1960s.

19. Here quoting the phrase associated with the "Responsibility to Protect" paragraphs from the 2005 World Summit Outcome document (A/RES/60/1), UN General Assembly, September 15, 2005, para. 138–139, http://www.unfpa.org/icpd/docs/2005summit_eng.pdf. In this document's exact, if convoluted, words: "The international community, through the United Nations, also has the responsibility to use appropriate diplomatic, humanitarian and other peaceful means, in accordance with Chapters VI and VIII of the Charter, to help to protect populations from genocide, war crimes, ethnic cleansing and

crimes against humanity. In this context, we are prepared to take collective action, in a timely and decisive manner, through the Security Council, in accordance with the Charter, including Chapter VII, on a case-by-case basis and in cooperation with relevant regional organizations as appropriate, should peaceful means be inadequate and national authorities are manifestly failing to protect their populations from genocide, war crimes, ethnic cleansing and crimes against humanity" (para. 139).

20.   See the Preamble to the Rome Statute of the International Criminal Court, adopted July 17, 1998, http://untreaty.un.org/cod/icc/index.html.

21.   See "Situations and cases," International Criminal Court (last accessed in September, 2009), http://www.icc-cpi.int/Menus/ICC/Situations+and+ Cases. Of these fourteen indictments and arrest warrants, five were against Ugandan members of the rebel Lord's Resistance Army (though one indictee has since died), five against nationals of the Democratic Republic of Congo, three against Sudanese nationals charged with prosecuting the government's counterinsurgency campaign in Darfur (including Sudan's President Omar Hassan Ahmad al Bashir), and a fourth one against a Sudanese national with the rebel United Resistance Front.

22.   See Philip Gourevitch, "The Life After," New Yorker, May 4, 2009; also see our Section 4, "Rwanda and the Democratic Republic of Congo," in the present work.

23.   See Final Judgment of the International Military Tribunal for the Trial of German Major War Criminals (September 30, 1946), http://avalon.law.yale.edu/subject_menus/judcont.asp, specifically "The Common Plan or Conspiracy and Aggressive War," http://avalon.law.yale.edu/imt/judnazi.asp#common, emphasis added.

24.   See "Human Rights Watch Policy on Iraq," undated statement, ca. late 2002 or early 2003, http://www.hrw.org/legacy/campaigns/iraq/hrwpolicy.htm. For a critique of Human Rights Watch, see Edward S. Herman, David Peterson, and George Szamuely, "Human Rights Watch in Service to the War Party," Electric Politics, February 26, 2007, http://www.electricpolitics.com/2007/02/human_rights_watch_in_service.html.

25.   John Ellis, The Social History of the Machine Gun (New York: Pantheon, 1973), 101.

26.   See Richard Seymour, The Liberal Defense of Murder (New York: Verso, 2008).

27.   According to Marc W. Herold at the University of New Hampshire: "Obama's Pentagon has been much more deadly for Afghan civilians

than was Bush's in comparable months of 2008. During January-June 2008, some 278–343 Afghan civilians perished at the hands of U.S./NATO forces, but for comparable months under Team Obama the numbers were 520–630." ("Afghanistan: Obama's unspoken trade-off," *Frontline* (India), August 29–September 11, 2009, http://www. hinduonnet.com/fline/stories/20090911261813000.htm.) Herold adds that under Obama, two other things have changed as well: The preponderance of U.S.-NATO violence has shifted from aerial attacks to attacks by ground forces; and the "public face of the war" has also shifted, from the rightly discredited George W. Bush, to someone more fluent in the language and imagery of American liberals.

28. Peter Baker, "Obama's Choice for U.N. Is Advocate of Strong Action Against Mass Killings," *New York Times*, December 1, 2008; Susan E. Rice, "Why Darfur Can't Be Left to Africa," *Washington Post*, August 7, 2005; Susan E. Rice, "Respect for International Humanitarian," USUN Press Release #020, U.S. Department of State, January 29, 2009.

29. See "Iraq War," International Coalition for the Responsibility to Protect, undated, http://www.responsibilitytoprotect.org/index. php/middle-east#1._the_iraq_war.

30. See the Interactive Thematic Dialogue of the United Nations General Assembly on the Responsibility to Protect, July 23, 2009, which includes the texts of the prepared statements by each of the six presenters, http://www.un.org/ga/president/63/interactive/responsibili-tytoprotect.shtml. Also see *Implementing the responsibility to protect: Report of the Secretary-General* (A/63/677), January 12, 2009, http://www.un.org/ga/search/view_doc.asp?symbol=A/63/677&Lang=E.

31. See Jean Bricmont, *Humanitarian Imperialism: Using Human Rights to Sell War*, trans. Diana Johnstone (New York: Monthly Review Press, 2006).

32. See Gareth Evans, *The Responsibility to Protect: Ending Mass Atrocity Crimes Once and For All* (Washington, D.C.: Brookings Institution Press, 2008).

33. See Gareth Evans, Mohamed Sahnoun, *et al.*, *The Responsibility To Protect*, Report of the International Commission on Intervention and State Sovereignty (Ottawa: International Development Research Centre, 2001), http://www.iciss.ca/menu-en.asp.

34. Our transcription, drawn from John Pilger's documentary, *Death of a Nation: The Timor Conspiracy*, 1994.

35. Our transcription, drawn from the 52-minute "Responsibility to Protect" Press Conference, United Nations, New York City, July 23,

2009, beginning at the 41:45 mark, http://webcast.un.org/ramgen/
ondemand/pressconference/2009/pc090723pm.rm.

36. In his book, Gareth Evans writes that as of mid-2008, the "clearest
prima facie candidates . . . for inclusion in . . . [an R2P] watch list . . .
[were] Burma/Myanmar, Burundi, China, Congo, Iraq, Kenya, Sri
Lanka, Somalia, Sudan, Uzbekistan, and Zimbabwe." (*The
Responsibility to Protect*, 76.) Evans does not spell out any reasons for
naming these eleven R2P candidates, nor does he name which victims
need to be protected from which perpetrators in each of these eleven
theaters. In reference to Iraq, Evans has long maintained that the 2003
U.S.–U.K. invasion could not have been justified on "humanitarian"
grounds, though he adds that it was a "close call." ("Humanity did not
justify this war," *Financial Times*, May 15, 2003.) But as with the
International Coalition for the Responsibility to Protect (see n. 27,
above) and many other R2P advocates, the only question that Evans
entertains is whether the violence of Iraqi national life was sufficient
to provide R2P-type justification for the ongoing foreign occupation
of Iraq. Left unasked is whether the Iraqis themselves may have ever
needed protection from the U.S. and U.K. invader-occupiers of their
country. Indeed, this is because it is an article of faith among R2P
advocates that the United States and the great Western powers possess a "responsibility to protect" the victims of non-Western perpetrators, but that the victims of the United States and its Western allies
have no recourse but to suffer their fate in silence or be labeled "terrorists" (and the like) for resisting. The bias evident here runs deep.

37. UN Security Council Resolution 660 of August 2, 1990 (S/RES/660)
demanded Iraq's withdrawal from Kuwait. Resolution 661 of August
6, 1990 (S/RES/661) imposed economic sanctions to enforce Iraq's
compliance with 660. But it was Resolution 687 of April 3, 1991
(S/RES/687, esp. para. 7-14) that called for the disarmament of Iraq's
WMD and created the Special Commission to supervise compliance.
Last, Resolution 1483 of May 22, 2003 (S/RES/1483) rescinded all
of the above, as the scramble for Iraq began.

38. Patrick E. Tyler, "U.S. Officials Believe Iraq Will Take Years to
Rebuild," *New York Times*, June 3, 1991; Barton Gellman, "Allied Air
War Struck Broadly in Iraq; Officials Acknowledge Strategy Went
Beyond Purely Military Targets," *Washington Post*, June 23, 1991.

39. "Protocol Additional to the Geneva Conventions of 12 August 1949,"
entered into force on December 7, 1979, Article 54, "Protection of
objects indispensable to the survival of the civilian population."
Therein we read: "1. Starvation of civilians as a method of warfare is
prohibited. 2. It is prohibited to attack, destroy, remove or render use-

less objects indispensable to the survival of the civilian population, such as foodstuffs, agricultural areas for the production of foodstuffs, crops, livestock, drinking water installations and supplies and irrigation works, for the specific purpose of denying them for their sustenance value to the civilian population or to the adverse Party, whatever the motive, whether in order to starve out civilians, to cause them to move away, or for any other motive." Here we note that the U.S. Government has never ratified this Protocol.

40. Thomas J. Nagy, "The Secret Behind the Sanctions: How the U.S. Intentionally Destroyed Iraq's Water Supply," *The Progressive*, September 2001, http://www.progressive.org/mag_nagysanctions. The International Study Team reported as early as October 1991 that "modern" Iraq had been destroyed. See *Health and Welfare in Iraq after the Gulf Crisis: An in-Depth Assessment*, October 1991. Also see Eric Herring, "Between Iraq and a hard place: a critique of the British government's case for UN economic sanctions," *Review of International Studies*, Vol. 28, No. 1, January, 2002; and Joy Gordon, "Economic Sanctions as a Weapon of Mass Destruction," *Harper's Magazine* November, 2002.

41. See the *Final reports of the 1st, 2nd and 3rd panels established pursuant to the note by the President of the Security Council of 30 Jan. 1999 (S/1999/100) concerning disarmament, monitoring and verification issues, the humanitarian situation in Iraq, and prisoners of war and Kuwaiti property* (S/1999/356), specifically Annex II, "Concerning the Current Humanitarian Situation in Iraq," esp. para. 43–51.

42. See "Iraq survey shows 'humanitarian emergency,'" UNICEF, Press Release, August 12, 1999, http://www.unicef.org/newsline/ 99pr29.htm. Also Peter L. Pellett, "Sanctions, Good Nutrition, and Health in Iraq," in Anthony Arnove, ed., *Iraq Under Siege: The Deadly Impact of Sanctions and War* (Boston: South End Press, 2000), 151–168.

43. Hans C. von Sponeck, *A Different Kind of War: The UN Sanctions Regime in Iraq* (New York: Berghahn Books, 2006), 52; n. 93, 47.

44. Hans C. von Sponeck, "Iraq—Twelve Years of Sanctions: Justified Punishment or Illegal Treatment?" Transnational Foundation for Peace and Future Research, December 6, 2002.

45. John Mueller and Karl Mueller, "Sanctions of Mass Destruction," *Foreign Affairs*, May/June 1999. "No one knows with any precision how many Iraqi civilians have died as a result," they add, "but various agencies of the United Nations, which oversees the sanctions, have estimated that they have contributed to hundreds of thousands of deaths."

46. "Punishing Saddam," *60 Minutes*, CBS TV, May 12, 1996.

47. For Table 1, Rows 1–7, the parameters we used for our Factiva database searches were:

Row 1: rst=**Iraq** and (**sanctions** w/5 genocid*) not (Afghanistan or Bosnia or Burundi or Cambodia or Congo or Darfur or East Timor or Ethiopia or Guatemala or Indonesia or Kosovo or Rwanda or Sudan or Turkey or Vietnam) for January 1, 1992, through December 31, 2008.

Row 2: rst=(**Iraq** w/5 genocid*) not (Afghanistan or Bosnia or Burundi or Cambodia or Congo or Darfur or East Timor or Ethiopia or Guatemala or Indonesia or Kosovo or Rwanda or Sudan or Turkey or Vietnam) for January 1, 2004, through December 31, 2008.

Row 3: rst=(**Bosnia** w/5 genocid*) not (Afghanistan or Burundi or Cambodia or Congo or Darfur or East Timor or Ethiopia or Guatemala or Indonesia or Iraq or Rwanda or Sudan or Turkey or Vietnam) for January 1, 1992, through December 31, 2008.

Row 4: rst=(**Kosovo** w/5 genocid*) not (Afghanistan or Burundi or Cambodia or Congo or Darfur or East Timor or Ethiopia or Guatemala or Indonesia or Iraq or Rwanda or Sudan or Turkey or Vietnam) for January 1, 1998, through December 31, 2008.

Row 5: rst=(**Rwanda** w/5 genocid*) not (Afghanistan or Bosnia or Burundi or Cambodia or Congo or Darfur or East Timor or Ethiopia or Guatemala or Indonesia or Iraq or Kosovo or Sudan or Turkey or Vietnam) from April 1, 1994, through December 31, 2008

Row 6: rst=(**Congo** w/5 genocid*) not (Afghanistan or Bosnia or Burundi or Cambodia or Darfur or East Timor or Ethiopia or Guatemala or Indonesia or Iraq or Kosovo or Rwanda or Sudan or Turkey or Vietnam) for January 1, 1998, through December 31, 2008.

Row 7: rst=(**Darfur** w/5 genocid*) not (Afghanistan or Bosnia or Burundi or Cambodia or Congo or East Timor or Ethiopia or Guatemala or Indonesia or Iraq or Kosovo or Rwanda or Turkey or Vietnam) for January 1, 2004, through December 31, 2008.

48. See, e.g., "The *Times* and Iraq," Editorial, *New York Times*, May 26, 2004, as well as the accompanying "Sample of the Coverage." Here we simply note that the case against the *Times* is far stronger than the *Times*'s editors admitted and that the body of relevant examples of the *Times*'s and the rest of the establishment media's role as advocates for the U.S. and U.K. war is far greater in scope than recognized by the *Times*.

49. Les Roberts *et al.*, "Mortality before and after the March 2003 invasion of Iraq: cluster sample survey," *The Lancet* (online), October 29, 2004; Gilbert Burnham *et al.*, "The Human Cost of the War in Iraq: A Mortality Study, 2002–2006," *The Lancet*, October 21, 2006; and

Munqith Daghir *et al.*, "New analysis 'confirms' 1 million + Iraqi casu-alties," Opinion Research Business, January 28, 2008. For electronic copies of these and related documents, see the Web site maintained by the Center for International Studies at MIT, *Iraq: The Human Cost*, http://web.mit.edu/humancostiraq/.

50. A search of the Factiva database (i.e., Iraq w/10 "supreme interna-tional crime") under the broadest "All Sources" category for the seven-year period January 1, 2002, through December 31, 2008, turned up a total of only six items in which someone referred to the U.S. war as an instance of a Nuremberg-class "supreme international crime." In the single most prominent of these, the former CIA analyst and member of Veteran Intelligence Professionals for Sanity Ray McGovern said over a U.S. television channel: "Nuremberg defined [aggression as] the supreme international crime, holding within itself the accumulated evil of the whole." From the immediate context, it is unmistakable that McGovern was referring to the U.S. war against Iraq. See *The News Hour with Jim Lehrer*, PBS–TV, April 24, 2006.

51. Howard Friel and Richard Falk, *The Record of the Paper: How the New York Times Misreports US Foreign Policy* (New York: Verso, 2004), 15.

52. "Statistics on Displaced Iraqis around the World," UN High-Commissioner for Refugees, September 2007; *Iraq: No Let-up in the Humanitarian Crisis*, International Committee of the Red Cross, March 2008; *Carnage and Despair: Iraq Five Years On*, Amnesty International, March 2008.

53. Douglas Jehl and Elizabeth Becker, "Experts' Pleas to Pentagon Didn't Save Museum," *New York Times*, April 16, 2003; Robson was referring to the looting of Iraq's National Museum just days before, under the watchful eyes of U.S. troops. For an assessment of the responsibility of the occupying army to protect Iraq's archeological sites, see Amy E. Miller, "The Looting of Iraqi Art: Occupiers and Collectors Turn Away Leisurely from the Disaster," *Case Western Reserve Journal of International Law*, Vol. 37, No. 1, 2005. Also Lawrence Rothfield, *The Rape of Mesopotamia: Behind the Looting of the Iraq Museum* (Chicago: University of Chicago Press, 2009).

54. See, e.g., Michael Smith, "The War Before the War," *New Statesman*, May 30, 2005.

55. See David Peterson, "British Records on the Prewar Bombing of Iraq," ZNet, July 6, 2005, http://www.zcommunications.org/british-records-on-the-prewar-bombing-of-iraq-by-david-peterson-1.

56. See David Peterson, "'Spikes of Activity,'" ZNet July 5, 2005, http://www.zcommunications.org/spikes-of-activity-by-david-peter-son-1. This catalogues the relevant Iraqi documents from December

16, 2001, through February 11–14, 2003, after which time the series was interrupted by the start of the war and the overthrow of the Iraqi government.

57. UN Security Council Resolution 1546 (S/RES/1546), June 8, 2004.

58. See Declaration of Principles for a Long-Term Relationship of Cooperation and Friendship Between the Republic of Iraq and the United States of America, White House Office of the Press Secretary, November 26, 2007, http://www.globalpolicy.org/component/content/article/168/36325.html; and Alissa Rubin and Campbell Robertson, "Iraq Approves Deal Charting End of U.S. Role," *New York Times*, November 28, 2008.

59. "Iraq opens its oil fields to foreign companies, 35 qualify," *Oil and Gas News*, November 30, 2008; "Northern Iraq Export Prospects Inch Forward," *Petroleum Intelligence Weekly*, December 1, 2008; Danny Fortson, "Oil giants are itching to invade Iraq," *Sunday Times* (U.K.), December 28, 2008; Patrick Cockburn, "Iraqi Oil Minister accused of mother of all sell-outs," *The Independent*, June 18, 2009; Gina Chon, "Big Oil Ready for Big Gamble in Iraq," *Wall Street Journal*, June 24, 2009; Sam Dagher, "Defiant Kurds Claim Oil, Gas and Territory," *New York Times*, July 10, 2009; Anthony Shadid, "Worries about a Kurdish-Arab Conflict Move to Fore in Iraq," *Washington Post*, July 27, 2009; and Patrick Cockburn, "Kurdish faultline threatens to spark new war," *The Independent*, August 10, 2009.

60. The first such comparison was by Lara Marlowe, "Whether occupation forces stay or go, there is going to be bloodshed," *Irish Times*, April 15, 2004. After the April 2004 assaults, Marlowe wrote: "In Falluja, US forces used fighter-bombers and attack helicopters against civilian areas for the first time since the fall of Saddam. In the mind of Iraqis, Falluja was a massacre representing something akin to Guernica in the Spanish Civil War, or Bloody Sunday in Northern Ireland."

61. "Senator hits out at Maliki, US embassy," Agence France Presse, October 1, 2007. Then a candidate for the U.S. presidency, Joe Biden was defending his blueprint for dividing Iraq into three self-governing territories.

62. Table 2 provides a more careful breakdown for the results in Table 1, Row 2. Only 13 items (Row 1) included the claim that Iraqi deaths during this period amount to a "genocide" the cause of which is the U.S. war and military occupation of Iraq. For the same period, 3 items (Row 2) claimed that genocide occurred in Iraq due to the 13-year sanctions regime; 48 items (Row 3) claimed the regime of Saddam Hussein was the perpetrator of genocide; and 54 items (Row 4)

claimed either that a sectarian conflict already had broken out in Iraq that is the cause of genocide, or that a genocidal conflict might break-out inside Iraq, were the occupying U.S. military to withdraw from the country. Last, there were 30 items (Row 5) that used the term "geno-cide" but did not attribute it to any of the other four categories—as when, for example, the *Chicago Sun-Times*'s Neil Steinberg mentioned "the bloodbath in Iraq, the genocide in Africa" ("Satan has nothing on monsters among us," October 30, 2006).

63. Samantha Power, "Dying in Darfur," *New Yorker*, August 30, 2004.
64. "Darfur rebels adopt charter to topple regime, create 'democratic Sudan,'" Agence France Presse, March 14, 2003.
65. "West Sudan's Darfur conflict 'world's greatest humanitarian crisis,'" Agence France Presse, March 19, 2004.
66. See Eric Reeves, "Unnoticed Genocide," *Washington Post*, February 25, 2004. Reeves repeated the same points in his Statement before the House International Relations Subcommittee on Africa, U.S. House of Representatives, March 11, 2004.
67. Kofi Annan to the UN Commission on Human Rights (SG/SM/9245), April 7, 2004, http://www.un.org/News/Press/docs/2004/sgsm9245.doc.htm.
68. Mahmood Mamdani, *Saviors and Survivors: Darfur, Politics, and the War on Terror* (New York: Pantheon, 2009), esp. "Arab Perpetrators and African Victims," 59–71; also see his "The Politics of Naming," *London Review of Books*, March 8, 2007, http://www.lrb.co.uk/v29/n05/mamd01.html.
69. Nicholas D. Kristof, "Will We Say 'Never Again' Yet Again?" *New York Times*, March 27, 2004. Also see Mamdani, *Saviors and Survivors*, n. 32, 310, and n. 36, 310–311.
70. Antonio Cassese *et al.*, *Report of the International Commission of Inquiry on Darfur to the United Nations Secretary-General* (S/2005/60), January 25, 2005, para. 508.
71. *Ibid.*, para. 510. Although this Commission took great pains to fit the conflicts in the western Sudan into the framework of the Genocide Convention, it could not accomplish this task, and in the end rejected any charge of genocide against the government in Khartoum.
72. Achim Steiner *et al.*, *Sudan: Post-Conflict Environmental Assessment*, UN Environment Program, 2007, http://www.unep.org/sudan, 329; Ban Ki-moon, "A Climate Culprit In Darfur," *Washington Post*, June 16, 2007; and David M. Cacarious Jr. *et al.*, *National Security and the Threat of Climate Change*, CNA Corporation, April, 2007, 15–20.
73. See "No End in Sight to Violence and Suffering in Sudan," Doctors Without Borders, part 8 of its annual *"Top Ten" Humanitarian Crises*

of 2008, December 22, 2008, http://www.doctorswithoutborders.org/press/release.cfm?id=3268%20.

74. See Mark Jones, "Tsunami coverage dwarfs 'forgotten' crises," Reuters-AlertNet, March 10, 2005, http://www.alertnet.org/the-facts/reliefresources/111044767025.htm, as well as the related charts and graphs for total press coverage during the period March 2004–February 2005. Eliminating the coverage given to the December 26, 2004, tsunami in the Indian Ocean (an act of nature), this study found that Darfur was the most heavily reported political-humanitarian crisis throughout the 12-month period.

75. John Prendergast, "Sudan's Ravines of Death," *New York Times*, July 15, 2004.

76. Steven Kull *et al.*, "Americans on the Crisis in Sudan," Program on International Policy Attitudes, July 20, 2004, http://www.pipa.org. A follow-up poll conducted six-months later simply assumed that genocide was occurring in Darfur, and asked respondents whether they believed that various combinations of military force (unilaterally by the United States, multilaterally by the Security Council) were appropriate to "stop the genocide in Darfur." Steven Kull *et al.*, "Three Out of Four Americans Favor UN Military Intervention in Darfur," Program on International Policy Attitudes, January 24, 2005.

77. Albright and Cohen, *Preventing Genocide*, 14.

78. Benjamin Coghlan *et al.*, *Mortality in the Democratic Republic of Congo: An Ongoing Crisis*, International Rescue Committee–Burnet Institute, January, 2008, ii. Also see the accompanying Press Release, January 22, 2008, http://www.theirc.org/news/irc-study-shows-congos0122.html. (See our section on "Rwanda and the Democratic Republic of Congo.")

79. Steven Fake and Kevin Funk, *The Scramble for Africa: Darfur—Intervention and the USA* (New York: Black Rose Books, 2009), esp. chap. 8, "Darfur Activism—Aiding the Victims or the Superpower?"

80. Andrew Heavens, "Sudan's Darfur no longer at war—peacekeeping chief," Reuters, August 27, 2009.

81. Neil MacFarquhar, "As Darfur Fighting Diminishes, U.N. Officials Focus on the South of Sudan," *New York Times*, August 28, 2009.

82. *Ibid.*

83. See the "About Us" function at the Enough Project, http://www.enoughproject.org/about (accessed in October 2009). As the opening paragraph explains: "The Enough Project is helping to build a permanent constituency to prevent genocide and crimes against humanity. Too often, the United States and the larger international community have taken a wait-and-see approach to crimes

against humanity. This is unconscionable." Of course, the Enough Project makes no mention of preventing mass-atrocity crimes when the United States and its allies are the perpetrators, rather than bystanders.

84. See the web page devoted to the "Keep the Promise: Sudan Now" campaign, where a list of six affiliated organizations is displayed across the bottom, http://www.sudanactionnow.com (accessed in October 2009).

85. Alex de Waal, "'Save Darfur': Fast the Eid!" *Making Sense of Darfur*, September 14, 2009, http://blogs.ssrc.org/darfur/2009/09/14/save-darfur-fasting-at-eid.

86. For several critical resources relevant to this and to the sections on Kosovo as well as Operation Storm, see Susan L. Woodward, *Balkan Tragedy: Chaos and Dissolution After the Cold War* (Washington, D.C.: Brookings Institution, 1995); Robert M. Hayden, *Blueprints for a House Divided: The Constitutional Logic of the Yugoslav Conflicts* (Ann Arbor, MI: University of Michigan Press, 1999); David Chandler, "Western Intervention and the Disintegration of Yugoslavia, 1989–1999," in Philip Hammond and Edward S. Herman, *Degraded Capability: The Media and the Kosovo Crisis* (Sterling, VI: Pluto Press, 2000), 19–30; Diana Johnstone, *Fools' Crusade: Yugoslavia, NATO and Western Delusions* (New York: Monthly Review Press, 2002); Peter Brock, *Media Cleansing: Dirty Reporting. Journalism and Tragedy in Yugoslavia* (Los Angeles: GM Books, 2005); and Edward S. Herman and David Peterson, "The Dismantling of Yugoslavia: A Study in Inhumanitarian Intervention," *Monthly Review* 59, September, 2007, http://www.monthlyreview.org/1007herman-peterson1.php.

87. LTC John E. Sray, "Selling the Bosnian Myth to America: Buyer Beware," Foreign Military Studies Office Publications, Department of the Army, October, 1995, http://fmso.leavenworth.army.mil/documents/bosnia2.htm.

88. See, e.g., Barry Schweid, "Bosnian Leader Appeals for U.S. Support," Associated Press, January 8, 1993. Schweid paraphrases Bosnian Muslim President Alija Izetbegovic, "frustrated in his call for U.S. military intervention," telling reporters at a news conference in New York that "some 200,000 people may have died in the former Yugoslav republic in nine months of pounding by Bosnian Serbs."

89. For the two principal studies, see Ewa Tabeau and Jakub Bijak, "War-related Deaths in the 1992–1995 Armed Conflicts in Bosnia and Herzegovina," *European Journal of Population*, Vol. 21, June 2005, 187–215; Tabeau-Bijak estimate 102,622 total war-related deaths on

all sides, of which 55,261 (54%) were civilian and 47,360 (46%) were combatants. Also see Patrick Ball *et al.*, *Bosnian Book of the Dead: Assessment of the Database*, Research and Documentation Center, Sarajevo, June, 2007, http://www.idc.org.ba/presentation/content. htm. These researchers (one of whom is Ewa Tabeau) estimate 97,207 deaths in all, of which 57,523 (59.2%) were military and 39,684 (40.8%) were civilian. They also provide breakdowns of deaths-by-ethnicity (see "Research Results" > "Bosnia and Herzegovina," Slide 35):

Adapted from Slide 35: Killed and missing by military status and ethnicity, 1991–1995:

	Bosniaks	Serbs	Croats	Others
Military	30,966	20,830	5,625	102
Civilian	33,070	4,075	2,163	376

90. See the *Judgment, Prosecutor v. Radislav Krstic* (IT-98-33-T), ICTY, August 2, 2001, para. 589–598.

91. Michael Mandel, *How America Gets Away with Murder: Illegal Wars, Collateral Damage, and Crimes Against Humanity* (Ann Arbor, MI: Pluto Press, 2004), 159.

92. See, e.g., George Szamuely, "Securing Guilty Verdicts: The Abuse of Witness Testimony at The Hague," in Edward S. Herman, ed., *The Srebrenica Massacre: Evidence, Context, Politics*, forthcoming.

93. See, e.g., Tim Judah and Daniel Sunter, "How the video that put Serbia in dock was brought to light," *The Observer*, June 5, 2005. Although the video itself ultimately was not admitted as evidence to the Milosevic trial, Judah and Sunter referred to the video as the "smoking gun"—"the final, incontrovertible proof of Serbia's part in the Srebrenica massacres in which more than 7,500 Bosnian Muslim men and boys were murdered."

94. The phrase "joint criminal enterprise" was first introduced by the ICTY's Prosecution in its Initial Indictment of Slobodan Milosevic in relation to Croatia (IT-01-54, September 27, 2001, para. 5-9), then extended to the Second Amended Indictment of Milosevic in relation to Kosovo (IT-99-37, October 16, 2001, para. 16-18), and, finally, for a third time, to the Initial Indictment of Milosevic for Bosnia and Herzegovina (IT-01-51, November 22, 2001, para. 5–9).

95. "U.N. war crimes tribunal launches Kosovo investigation," Deutsche Presse-Agentur, March 10, 1998; Philip Shenon, " U.S. Dispatches Its Balkans Mediator with a Warning to the Serbs," *New York Times*, May 9, 1998.

96. On covert aid to the KLA, see, e.g., Tom Walker and Aidan Laverty,

"CIA aided Kosovo guerrilla army," *Sunday Times*, March 12, 2000; Peter Beaumont *et al.*, "'CIA's bastard army ran riot in Balkans,'" *The Observer*, March 11, 2001; James Bissett, "We created a monster," *Toronto Globe and Mail*, July 31, 2001.

97. George Robertson, Testimony before the Select Committee on Defense, U.K. House of Commons, March 24, 1999, para. 391. Robertson's exact words were: "Up until Račak earlier this year the KLA were responsible for more deaths in Kosovo than the Yugoslav authorities had been."

98. For the 2,000-figure, see, e.g., "Mutilated Bodies Found after Serb Attack," *New York Times*, January 17, 1999; Barton Gellman, "U.S., Allies Order Attack on Serbia," *Washington Post*, March 24, 1999.

99. Population flows in Kosovo prior to and during NATO's 1999 bombing war correlated, not with a plan of ethnic cleansing and forced expulsion, but with strategic military factors, including the intensity of fighting, the operational presence of the KLA in the various theaters of combat, and the relative density of the national groups living in the areas being contested. Across Kosovo's twenty-nine municipalities, ethnic Albanians did not flee the territory uniformly. Nor were they alone—members of all ethnic groups fled areas where fighting took place. Municipalities in different parts of Kosovo where the KLA's presence was thin saw relatively little fighting and therefore little refugee flow. This was particularly true prior to the start of NATO's bombing war on March 24, 1999. See the report published by the OSCE, *Kosovo/Kosova: As Seen, As Told. The human rights findings of the OSCE Kosovo Verification Mission October 1998 to June 1999*, esp. Part III, Ch. 14, "Forced Expulsion," 146–162; and Part V, "The Municipalities," 226–585, http://www.asylumlaw.org/docs/kosovo/ osce99_kosovo_asseenastold.pdf. Also see the treatment of this matter in Noam Chomsky, *A New Generation Draws the Line: Kosovo, East Timor and the Standards of the West* (Verso, 2000), 114 ff. Chomsky summarizes the work of former *New York Times* reporter David Binder, who "notes 'a curiosity' documented in the OSCE report: 46 percent of the Albanians left Kosovo during the bombing, along with 60 percent of the Serbians and Montenegrins. Thus, 'proportionately more Serbs were displaced during the bombing, and they did not return to Kosovo'" (114). Last, see the testimony of late British journalist Eve-Ann Prentice during the defense phase of the trial of Slobodan Milosevic. Asked her opinion about why so many Kosovo Albanians fled the province during NATO's bombing war, Prentice said, variously, "we were told many times that . . . ordinary civilian ethnic Albanians . . . had been told it was their patriotic duty to leave

because the world was watching . . . and that anybody who failed to join this exodus was somehow not supporting the—the Albanian cause. . . . [T]hey had been told by KLA leaders that their patriotic duty was to join the exodus, was to leave Kosovo, to be seen to be leaving Kosovo." (Testimony of Eve-Ann Prentice, *Prosecutor v. Slobodan Milosevic* (IT-02-54), February 3, 2006, 47908–47909.)

100. George Jahn, "Charges of Kosovo genocide as NATO bolsters forces," Associated Press, March 28, 1999.

101. "Ethnic Cleansing in Kosovo," U.S. Department of State, April 19, 1999, http://www.state.gov/www/regions/eur/rpt_990416_ksvo_ethnic.html. Under the heading "Detentions," this news release stated: "We are gravely concerned about the fate of the missing men. Their number ranges from a low of 100,000, looking only at the men missing from among refugee families in Albania, up to nearly 500,000, if reports of widespread separation of men among the IDPs within Kosovo are true."

102. For the "Operation Horseshoe" story, see R. Jeffrey Smith and William Drozdiak, "Serbs' Offensive Was Meticulously Planned," *Washington Post*, April 11, 1999; for the Hashim Thaci story, see Marie Colvin *et al.*, "Slaughter of the Innocents," *Sunday Times*, April 4, 1999; and for remarks by Secretary of Defense William Cohen, see Bob Schieffer, *Face The Nation*, CBS-TV, May 16, 1999. Finally, for a debunking of "Operation Horseshoe," see Heinz Loquai, *Der Kosovo-Konflikt. Wege in einen vermeidbaren Krieg* (Baden-Baden: Nomos, 2000). In English, Loquai's title translates as "The Kosovo Conflict: The War that Could Have Been Avoided."

103. Marlise Simons, "Investigators from Many Nations to Begin Search for War Crimes," *New York Times*, June 15, 1999; Julian Borger, "Cook promises to make killers pay; Scenes of mass murder vindicate Nato, says foreign secretary," *The Guardian*, June 24, 1999.

104. See Carla Del Ponte, "Statement to the Press by Carla Del Ponte" (FH/P.I.S./550-e), International Criminal Tribunal for the Former Yugoslavia, December 20, 2000, para. 16, http://www.un.org/icty/pressreal/p550-e.htm; and the International Committee of the Red Cross, "Kosovo: ICRC publishes new edition of 'Book of the Missing,'" August 29, 2007, http://www.icrc.org/web/eng/siteeng0.nsf/htmlall/kosovo-news-290807?opendocument.

105. Herman and Peterson, "The Dismantling of Yugoslavia," 1.

106. Allison Des Forges *et al.*, *"Leave None to Tell the Story": Genocide in Rwanda* (New York: Human Rights Watch, 1999), specifically "The Attack on Habyarimana," 5–6, 185.

107. See *Prosecutor v. Augustin Ndindiliyimana et al.* (or *Military II*)

(ICTR-00-56-I), Transcript, September 19, 2006, 4, lines 13–22.
108. For the extended testimony of Prosecution witness Alison Des
Forges, see *Prosecutor v. Augustin Ndindiliyimana et al.*, September 18,
2006, through October 16, 2006, which produced a total of seventeen
days of testimony. Given that Rwanda's civilian intelligence services
were in the hands of a pro-Rwandan Patriotic Front minister, three
consecutive prime ministers under a power-sharing accord had been
either pro-RPF or subsidized by it, and Rwanda's "integrated" military
then combined the armed forces of the Tutsi-led RPF that was seeking the overthrow of the government alongside the government's regular army, the cross-examination of Des Forges from September 21
on shows her failing to support the standard model of the "Rwandan
genocide" at every turn.
109. Alison Des Forges died in a commuter plane crash on February 12,
2009, while returning to her home in Buffalo, New York. An obituary
written by Human Rights Watch Executive Director Kenneth Roth
praised his longtime colleague for "her central role in the prosecution
of the Hutus" ("A Heroine for Human Rights," *Huffington Post*,
February 15, 2009). It is true that Des Forges acted energetically on
behalf of the Prosecution at the ICTR and in similar venues against
the Hutu in general, but the perception of her "expertise" flowed less
from her knowledge of Rwanda than her tirelessness as an advocate
for the standard model of the "Rwandan genocide" and the thorough-
ness with which this model has been institutionalized in the United
States and Britain. In 1991, Des Forges went to Rwanda on behalf of
the U.S. government and, in her own words, "attempted to put my
knowledge into a policy-oriented framework." "What was new was the
relationship to the United States government," she explained. Later,
"I went to Rwanda in July of '92 as a consultant to the United States
government, again for the same democracy project. Then I went back
in the first part of January '93 as the co-chair of an international commission to investigate human rights abuses in Rwanda." (Here quoting Des Forges' testimony in *Prosecutor of the Tribunal Against Jean
Paul Akayasu* (ICTR-96-4), Transcript, February 12, 1997,
112–114.) As the real policy of the U.S. government from at least
1990 on was regime change in Rwanda, namely, the ouster of the
Hutu government by the RPF, as well as the ouster of France from the
region (France had backed the Hutu government), we can easily see
how Des Forges' work from 1991 on helped provide cover for the U.S.
takeover of as many as four countries via its proxies in Uganda and the
RPF in Rwanda. In short, Alison Des Forges' career is best understood in terms of the services she performed on behalf of U.S. power

projection in Central Africa, with this policy-oriented work couched in the rhetoric of "human rights." In the process, Des Forges badly misinformed a whole generation of scholars, activists, and the cause of peace and justice as well.

110. See Jonathan Clayton, "Rwanda to appeal to UN Security Council on rebel invasion," Reuters, October 15, 1990; UN Security Council Resolution 812 (S/RES/812), March 12, 1993; and UN Security Council Resolution 846 (S/RES/846), June 22, 1993.

111. For compelling evidence on this point, see Robin Philpot, *Rwanda 1994: Colonialism Dies Hard* (E-Text as posted to the Taylor Report Website, 2004), esp. Chap. 1–7, http://www.taylor-report.com/Rwanda_1994.

112. Herman J. Cohen, *Intervening in Africa: Superpower Peacemaking in a Troubled Continent* (New York: St. Martin's Press, 2000), 177–178.

113. See Philpot, *Rwanda 1994: Colonialism Dies Hard*, esp. the "Conclusion."

114. See the Peace Agreement between the Government of the Republic of Rwanda and the Rwandese Patriotic Front, signed at Arusha on August 4 1993, U.N. General Assembly (A/48/824-S/26915), December 23, 1993. A total of seven documents were gathered together as the "Arusha Peace Accords," the earliest the N'Sele Cease-fire Agreement dating from 1991.

115. See *Judgment, The Prosecutor v. Théoneste Bagosora et al.* (ICTR-98-41-T), International Criminal Tribunal for Rwanda, December 18, 2008, http://69.94.11.53/ENGLISH/cases/Bagosora/judgement.htm. The four defendants in this case were: "Colonel Théoneste Bagosora, the directeur de cabinet of the Ministry of Defence, General Gratien Kabiligi, the head of the operations bureau (G-3) of the army general staff, Major Aloys Ntabakuze, the commander of the elite Para Commando Battalion, and Colonel Anatole Nsengiyumva, the commander of the Gisenyi operational sector" (para. 1).

116. *Ibid.*, para. 13, quoting from the oral summary of the case read in court the day the verdict was delivered. For the *Judgment*'s full discussion of the acquittal on this charge, see Sect. 2.1, "Conspiracy to Commit Genocide," para. 2084–2112.

117. Allan C. Stam, "Coming to a New Understanding of the Rwanda Genocide," a lecture before the Gerald R. Ford School of Public Policy, University of Michigan, February 18, 2009, our transcription, http://www.fordschool.umich.edu/news/events/?event_id=154.

118. "Rwandan embassy closed, U.S. seeks to remove Rwanda from UN Council," Agence France Presse, July 15, 1994; "Clinton Orders Nonstop Aid Flights for Rwandan Victims," Associated Press, July 22,

1994; "U.S. recognizes new government in Rwanda," Reuters, July 29, 1994; "200 U.S. troops going into Kigali to open airport," Reuters, July 29, 1994.

119. See UN Security Council Resolution 912 (S/RES/912), April 21, 1994, para. 8. The force levels of the UN Assistance Mission in Rwanda were reduced to a target of 270 infantry, down from 1515 on April 20, and 2165 as of April 6. In the words of Rwandan UN Ambassador Jean-Damascène Bizimana: "[T]he international community does not seem to have acted in an appropriate manner to reply to the anguished appeal of the people of Rwanda. This question has often been examined from the point of view of the ways and means to withdraw [UNAMIR], without seeking to give the appropriate weight to the concern of those who have always believed, rightly, that, in view of the security situation now prevailing in Rwanda, UNAMIR's members should be increased to enable it to contribute to the re-establishment of the cease-fire and to assist in the establishment of security conditions that could bring an end to the violence. . . .The option chosen by the Council, reducing the number of troops in UNAMIR . . . , is not a proper response to this crisis. . . ." "The situation concerning Rwanda," UN Security Council (S/PV.3368), April 21, 1994, 6.

120. Raymond Bonner, "U.N. Stops Returning Rwandan Refugees," *New York Times*, September 18, 1994. Also see Chris McGreal and Edward Luce, "Death Threats Force Out Aid Workers," *The Guardian*, October 3, 1994; Jean-Michel Stoullig, "UN spotlights claims of summary Rwandan reprisal killings," Agence France Presse, October 4, 1994.

121. See the treatment of the Gersony Report in Des Forges, *"Leave None to Tell the Story,"* specifically "The Gersony Mission," 726–732, which reproduces the UNHCR letter stating that the Gersony Report "does not exist" (727).

122. See the recollection of a meeting with Robert Gersony in Gérard Prunier, *Africa's World War: Congo, the Rwandan Genocide, and the Making of a Continental Catastrophe* (New York: Oxford University Press, 2009), 15–16; and n. 59–62, 373. As Prunier describes it: "Gersony's conclusion was that between early April and mid-September 1994 the RPF had killed between 25,000 and 45,000 people, *including Tutsis*. The UNHCR, which had commissioned the study for quite a different purpose, was appalled" (16).

123. George E. Moose, "Human Rights Abuses in Rwanda," Information Memorandum to The Secretary, U.S. Department of State, undated though clearly drafted between September 17 and 20, 1994. This document was called to our attention by Peter Erlinder, the director of the Rwanda Documents Project at William Mitchell College of Law,

St. Paul, Minnesota, ICTR Military-1 Exhibit, DNT 264, http://www.rwandadocumentsproject.net/gsdl/collect/mil1docs/i ndex/assoc/HASH8152.dir/doc84139.PDF.

124. Christian Davenport and Allan Stam, *Rwandan Political Violence in Space and Time*, unpublished manuscript, 2004 (available at Davenport's personal website: http://www.cdavenport.com). For all of Rwanda from April through July 1994, these authors report a total of 1,063,336 deaths (28), based on their analysis of a minimum of eight different mortality estimates for the relevant period.

125. *Ibid.*, see esp. 30–33.

126 Christian Davenport and Allan C. Stam, "What Really Happened in Rwanda?" *Miller-McCune*, October 6, 2009, http://www.miller-mccune.com/culture_society/what-really-happened-in-rwanda-1504.

127. In 1999, former RPF military officer Christophe Hakizimana submitted a letter to the UN Commission of Inquiry into the actions of the United Nations during the 1994 genocide in Rwanda (Ingvar Carlsson *et al.*), which detailed the RPF's military strategy from 1990 on. In his letter, Hakizimana claimed that the RPF was responsible for killing as many as two million Hutu in Rwanda and the Democratic Republic of Congo, and he informed the Commission that by indicting Hutu, the ICTR was focusing on the wrong side in the conflict. We base this on personal communications with the international criminal lawyer Christopher Black of Toronto, who, since 2000, has served as defense counsel before the ICTR on behalf of the Hutu General Augustin Nindiliyimana, a former Chief of Staff of the Rwanda Gendarmerie (or National Police).

128. For a more critical discussion of these issues, see Stam, "Coming to a New Understanding of the Rwanda Genocide," and our discussion of this above.

129. See Davenport and Stam, *Rwandan Political Violence in Space and Time*. Davenport and Stam organize their work according to three "jurisdictions" that we find deeply flawed: Namely, territory controlled by the Rwandan government and army, by the Rwandan Patriotic Front, and territory that falls along the lines of battle between the two. They write that "the actor with the greatest monopoly of coercion within a specific locale is generally held to be responsible for violent behavior in that locale" (25). (Also see Figure 1, "1994 Rwandan Political Violence: Total Deaths by Troop Control," 29.) On the basis of this problematic assumption, Davenport and Stam contend that as "the majority of deaths took place within areas under the control of [the Rwandan government and army]—totaling

891,295"—the government and army are responsible for these deaths, which "could be classified" as genocide, among other possible crimes (28). But as the RPF in fact moved rapidly and decisively from battlefield success to control of the entire country, it is frankly counterintuitive to treat the badly outgunned, outmaneuvered, and ultimately routed government forces as in control of anything. On the contrary, the chief responsibility for Rwandan political violence in 1994 lay with the RPF and its project of driving the coalition government from power and seizing the Rwandan state.

130. Davenport and Stam, "What Really Happened in Rwanda?"

131. Affidavit of Michael Andrew Hourigan, International Criminal Tribunal for Rwanda, November 27, 2006, http://www.opjdr. org/Human%20rights_files/AFFIDAVIT%20OF%20MICHAEL% 20ANDREW%20HOURIGAN.htm. For other sources that discuss the suppression of the Hourigan memorandum, see Robin Philpot, *Rwanda 1994*, esp. chap. 6, "It shall be called a plan crash"; Mark Colvin, "Questions unanswered 10 years after Rwandan genocide," PM, Australian Broadcasting Corporation, March 30, 2004, http://www.abc.net.au/pm/content/2004/s1077423.htm; Mark Doyle, "Rwanda 'plane crash halted,'" BBC News, February 9, 2007, http://news.bbc.co.uk/2/hi/africa/6348815.stm; and Nick McKenzie, "UN 'shut down' Rwanda probe," *The Age*, February 10, 2007, http://www.theage.com.au/news/world/un-shut-down-rwanda-probe/2007/02/09/1170524298428.html.

132. Richard Goldstone's remarks were reported by the Danish newspaper *Berlingske Tidende*. We are taking them from "ICTR/Attack—April 6th 1994 Attack Fits the ICTR's Mandate (Goldstone)," Hirondelle News Agency, December 13, 2006.

133. See Philpot, *Rwanda 1994*, chap. 6, "It shall be called a plane crash."

134. See Jean-Louis Bruguière, Request for the Issuance of International Arrest Warrants, Tribunal de Grande Instance, Paris, France, November 21, 2006, 15-16 (para. 100–103), http://www.olny. nl/RWANDA/Lu_Pour_Vous/ Dossier_Special_Habyarimana/ Rapport_Bruguiere.pdf.

135. Andrew England, "Rwanda president faces arrest," *Financial Times*, November 22, 2006; Chris McGreal, "French judge accuses Rwandan President of assassination," *The Guardian*, November 22, 2006; Fergal Keane, "Will we ever learn the truth about this genocide?" *The Independent*, November 22, 2006.

136. Findings based on both Factiva (*tnwp*) and NewsBank searches from January 1, 2000, through December 31, 2008. The sole truly serious effort in a U.S. newspaper to report and analyze both Michael

Hourigan's and Judge Bruguière's work was Sebastian Rotella, "French Magistrate Posits Theory on Rwandan Assassination," *Los Angeles Times*, February 17, 2007 (later reprinted in the *Seattle Times*).

137. Findings based on both Factiva (*tnwp*) and NewsBank searches from January 1, 2000, through December 31, 2008. Using the Factiva database to search the *New York Times*, *Wall Street Journal*, and *Washington Post* for mentions of the name "Bruguière," we found approximately one hundred items; but when we narrowed this search down to Bruguière's work in relation to Rwanda, we found only five items in all. Likewise with the NewsBank database for all U.S. newspapers: Bruguière's work was reported in well over four hundred items, but his work in relation to Rwanda in only seventeen.

138. Carla Del Ponte, with Chuck Sudetic, *Madame Prosecutor: Confrontations with Humanity's Worst Criminals and the Culture of Impunity: A Memoir* (New York: Other Press, 2009), esp. chap. 9, "Confronting Kigali: 2002 and 2003," 223–241. Also see Steven Edwards, "Del Ponte says UN caved to Rwandan pressure," *National Post*, September 17, 2003.

139. "Interview with Carla Del Ponte—'If I Had Had the Choice, I Would Have Remained Prosecutor of the ICTR,'" Hirondelle News Agency, September 16, 2003.

140. See Florence Hartmann, *Paix et Châtiment: Les Guerres Secrètes de la Politique et de la Justice Internationales* (Paris: Flammarion, 2007), 261–275.

141. "ICTR/Military I—Dallaire Wanted Americans to Investigate on Presidential Plane Crash," Hirondelle News Agency, February 9, 2004. In one illustration of Jallow's foot-dragging, he told the UN Security Council in December 2005 that the "allegations made against the Rwandan Patriotic Front have also been under consideration. Following the evaluation of the results of earlier investigations, it has become necessary to carry out additional inquiries into these allegations." (UN Security Council (S/PV.5328), December 15, 2005, 14.) But Jallow's "additional inquiries" were strictly *pro forma*, and the same delaying tactics served him through the end of 2008, at which date, no member of the RPF had ever been indicted by the ICTR, notwithstanding the chief prosecutor's "additional inquiries."

142. For the International Criminal Tribunal for Rwanda's founding Statute, see the Annex to UN Security Council Resolution 955 (S/RES/955), November 8, 1994, http://www.ictr.org/ENG-LISH/basicdocs/statute/ 2007.pdf. For a complete list of every case ever to have been indicted by the ICTR, see "Status of Cases," http://www.ictr.org/ENGLISH/cases/status.htm.

NOTES TO PAGES 63-65

143. Philip Gourevitch, *We wish to inform you that tomorrow we will be killed with our families: Stories from Rwanda* (New York: Picador, 1998), 225. Gourevitch concludes: "Kagame had proven himself quite effective at getting what he wanted, and if Kagame truly wanted to find an original response to his original circumstances, the only course open to him was emancipation. That was certainly how he presented it, and I didn't doubt that that was what he wanted" (226).

144. Stephen Kinzer, *A Thousand Hills: Rwanda's Rebirth and the Man Who Dreamed It* (Hoboken, NJ: John Wiley & Sons, 2008). Here we are quoting Kinzer's own words from a two-minute promotional video that his publisher circulated in 2008. At the hagiographic extreme for the literature on Paul Kagame and Rwanda, every chapter of Kinzer's book is introduced by quotes from Kagame ("For me, human rights is about everything," chap. 18). "Kagame is the man of the hour in modern Africa," Kinzer writes. "The eyes of all who hope for a better Africa are upon him. No other leader has made so much out of so little, and none offers such encouraging hope for the continent's future" (337).

145. Power, *"A Problem from Hell,"* 334–335. Also see Power, "Bystanders to Genocide," *The Atlantic,* September 2001.

146. See the statement by the Rwandan UN Ambassador Jean-Damascène Bizimana in n. 119, above.

147. See *Special Report of the Secretary-General on the United Nations Assistance Mission for Rwanda* (S/1994/470), April 20, 1994, specifically "Alternative 1," para. 13-14, which Boutros-Ghali himself endorsed.

148. Boutros Boutros-Ghali, *Unvanquished: A U.S.–U.N. Saga* (New York: Random House, 1999), 129–141. According to Robin Philpot, Boutros-Ghali told him on the record that "The genocide in Rwanda was 100 percent the responsibility of the Americans!" See the Introduction to Philpot, *Rwanda 1994.*

149. See Herman, Peterson, and Szamuely, "Human Rights Watch in Service to the War Party," http://www.electricpolitics.com/2007/02/human_rights_watch_in_service.html.

150. See *Report of the International Commission of Inquiry into human rights violations in Rwanda since October 1, 1990* (New York, March 1993). Besides Africa Watch (Human Rights Watch, USA), the other NGOs behind this commission were the International Federation of Human Rights Leagues (France), the Inter-African Union for Human Rights and the Rights of Peoples, and the International Center for Human Rights and Democratic Development (Canada).

151. *Ibid.* In a section titled "The Question of Genocide," after laying out Article II of the Genocide Convention, the Commission concluded

that "many Rwandans have been killed for the sole reason that they were Tutsi," although it added that "casualty figures . . . may be below the threshold required to establish genocide" (29). Besides Africa Watch (Human Rights Watch, USA), the other NGOs behind this commission were the International Federation of Human Rights Leagues (France), the Inter-African Union for Human Rights and the Rights of Peoples, and the International Center for Human Rights and Democratic Development (Canada).

152. Des Forges, *"Leave None to Tell the Story,"* 93.

153. Philpot, *Rwanda 1994,* chap. 4, "Scouts at Her Majesty's Service."

154. Linda Melvern, *A People Betrayed: The Role of the West in Rwanda's Genocide* (New York: Zed Books, 2000), 56.

155. "Rwanda: Report blames government for mass slayings," Inter Press Service, March 8, 1993.

156. See n. 78, above.

157. Filip Reyntjens' January 11, 2005 letter of resignation to Hassan Jallow is quoted in John Laughland, *A History of Political Trials: From Charles I to Saddam Hussein* (New York: Peter Lang Ltd., 2008), 211. The Reyntjens letter continued: "Article 6(2) of the [ICTR's] Statute explicitly rules out immunity, including for Heads of state or government or for responsible government officials. This principle is contravened when, as is currently the case, a message is sent out that those in power need not fear prosecution" (211–212).

158. The phrase "one tsunami every six months" was used in reference to the eastern Congo by then-head of the UN Office for the Coordination of Humanitarian Affairs Jan Egeland, based on the belief at the time that the December 26, 2004, tsunami in the Indian Ocean had taken 300,000 lives. Hence, in Egeland's words: "In terms of the human lives lost . . . this is the greatest humanitarian crisis in the world today and it is beyond belief that the world is not paying more attention." In Robert Evans, "UN Sees East Congo as Worse Crisis than Darfur," Reuters-AlertNet, March 16, 2005.

159. See the final two reports by Mahmoud Kassem *et al.* of the UN Panel of Experts on the Illegal Exploitation of Natural Resources and Other Forms of Wealth of the Democratic Republic of the Congo: S/2002/1146, October 8, 2002 (para. 152-153, 12); and S/2003/1027, October 15, 2003. Also see Björn Aust and Willem Jaspers, *From Resource War to "Violent Peace": Transition in the Democratic Republic of Congo,* Bonn International Center for Conversion, Paper No. 50, 2006. These authors note that approximately one-third of the earth's known cobalt deposits, and two-thirds of its known columbo tantalite (coltan) deposits, are to be found in

the DRC (Appendix 2, 149).

160. See Noam Chomsky, *Fateful Triangle: The United States, Israel, and the Palestinians* (Cambridge, MA: South End Press, Updated Ed., 1999), esp. chap. 5, "Peace for Galilee," 181–328.

161. Amnon Kapeliouk, *Sabra and Shatila: Inquiry into a Massacre*, Trans. Khalil Jahshan (Belmont, MA: Association of Arab-American University Graduates, 1984), 8.

162. *Ibid.*, 12, 14, 16.

163. *Ibid.*, 23, 30–31, 86. Israel's official Report of the Israeli Commission of Inquiry (Kahan Commission) estimated upwards of eight hundred Palestinians massacred in the two refugee camps. See "Excerpts from Report on Israel's Responsibility in Massacre," *New York Times*, February 9, 1983. Kapeliouk estimated that "Between 3,000–3,500 men, women and children were massacred within 48 hours between September 16 and 18, 1982," of which "approximately one-fourth of the victims were Lebanese, and the rest Palestinians" (63). For more on the Kahan Commission's whitewash of the massacre, see n. 166, below.

164. For Table 3, Rows 1–13, the parameters we used for our Factiva database searches were:

Row 1: rst=tnwp and (**Mozote** w/5 massacre)
Row 1: rst=tnwp and (**Mozote** w/10 genocid*)
Row 2: rst=tnwp and (**Rio Negro** w/5 massacre)
Row 2: rst=tnwp and (**Rio Negro** w/10 genocid*)
Row 3: rst=tnwp and ((**Sabra** or **Shatila**) w/5 massacre)
Row 3: rst=tnwp and (**Sabra** or **Shatila**) w/10 genocid*)
Row 4: rst=tnwp and (**Halabja** w/5 massacre)
Row 4: rst=tnwp and (**Halabja** w/10 genocid*)
Row 5: rst=tnwp and (Bosnia and (**market*** w/5 massacre))
Row 5: rst=tnwp and (Bosnia and (**market*** w/10 genocid*))
Row 6: rst=tnwp and (**Srebrenica** w/5 massacre)
Row 6: rst=tnwp and (**Srebrenica** w/10 genocid*)
Row 7: rst=tnwp and ((**Operation Storm** or **Krajina**) w/5 massacre)
Row 7: rst=tnwp and ((**Operation Storm** or **Krajina**) w/10 genocid*)
Row 8: rst=tnwp and (**Račak** w/5 massacre)
Row 8: rst=tnwp and (**Račak** w/10 genocid*)
Row 9: rst=tnwp and (**Liquiçá** w/5 massacre)
Row 9: rst=tnwp and (**Liquiçá** w/10 genocid*)
Row 10: rst=tnwp and (**Dasht** w/5 massacre)
Row 10: rst=tnwp and (**Dasht** w/10 genocid*)
Row 11: rst=tnwp and (**Falluja*** w/5 massacre)
Row 11: rst=tnwp and (**Falluja*** w/10 genocid*)

Row 12: rst=tnwp and (**Gaza** w/5 massacre)

Row 12: rst=tnwp and (**Gaza** w/10 genocid*) [checked carefully]

165. "Yasir Arafat, the chairman of the Palestine Liberation Organization, was quoted today as saying that his group was sending personnel and weapons back into southern Lebanon. 'We have the right after Sabra and Shatila and other genocides to help our people protect themselves, and to help the Lebanese people protect themselves', the English-language newspaper *Arab News* quoted Mr. Arafat as saying in an interview. 'So it is our duty and right'." ("PLO Sends Arms, Arafat Says," AP, *New York Times*, July 27, 1985. This AP report was also printed in the *Toronto Globe and Mail*, July 27, 1985.)

166. As Noam Chomsky has written: "[T]he Commission presents sufficient evidence that the top [Israeli] leadership fully expected a massacre when they sent the Phalange into the camps. They justified entry into West Beirut as an effort to prevent a Phalange massacre, and then proceeded to send the Phalange into the homes of their worst enemies—but with no intent to harm the population, the Commission 'asserts' without equivocation. Again, one can only conclude that the Report is designed for true believers, not for people capable of independent thought." *Fateful Triangle*, 397–410.

167. See the *Judgment, Prosecutor v. Radislav Krstic* (IT-98-33-T), August 2, 2001, para. 590.

168. See UN General Assembly Resolution 37/123 (A/RES/37/123), Section D, para. 2, December 16, 1982. But as the Israeli novelist Yitzhar Smilanski wrote at the time: "We have released famished lions into the arena. They devoured the people, therefore, the lions are the guilty party."

169. Jacques Clement, "'Ten times worse than an earthquake' in Gaza," Agence France Presse, January 19, 2009.

170. *Gaza: 1.5 million people trapped in despair*, International Committee of the Red Cross, June 29, 2009, http://www.icrc.org/Web/eng/siteeng0.nsf/htmlall/palestine-report-260609/$File/gaza-report-ICRC-eng.pdf.

171. John Dugard *et al.*, *No Safe Place, Report of the Independent Fact Finding Committee on Gaza*, League of Arab States, April 30, 2009, http://www.arableagueonline.org/las/picture_gallery/reportfullFI NAL.pdf. Also see *Israel/Gaza: Operation "Cast Lead": 22 days of death and destruction*, Amnesty International, July 2009, http://www.amnesty. org/en/library/asset/MDE15/015/2009/en/8f299083-9a74-4853-860f-0563725e633a/mde150152009en.pdf.

172. See "UN urged to 'find truth' about Gaza conflict," Amnesty International, March 16, 2009; and Amira Hass, "Judges, scholars call

on UN to probe war crimes by both sides in Gaza," *Haaretz*, March 20, 2009. Among this open letter's signatories were Amnesty International, South African Archbishop Desmond Tutu, the Irish former UN High Commissioner for Human Rights Mary Robinson, and the South African judge Richard Goldstone.

173. Ban Ki-moon, *Letter dated 4 May 2009 from the Secretary-General to the President of the Security Council: Summary by the Secretary-General of the report of the United Nations Headquarters Board of Inquiry into certain incidents in the Gaza Strip between 27 December 2008 and 19 January 2009,* (A/63/855–S/2009/250), 2. Also see "Beholden to the Big Powers: Israel, Gaza and the UN," *Media Lens* (U.K.), May 18, 2009, http://www.medialens.org/alerts/09/090518_beholden_to_the.php.

174. Ben Smith, "Obama-era goodwill for Rice at U.N.," *Politico.com*, April 4, 2009. In Susan Rice's words, by rejoining the Human Rights Council, "We are much better placed to be fighting for the principles we believe in—protection of human rights universally, fighting against the anti-Israel crap and for meaningful action on issues that we care about and ought to be the top of the agenda, things like Zimbabwe, Sudan [and] Burma."

175. "Recognizing Israel's right to defend itself against attacks from Gaza, reaffirming the United States' strong support for Israel, and supporting the Israel–Palestinian peace process" (H.Res. 34), U.S. House of Representatives, January 9, 2009. For the comments made from the floor of the U.S. Senate, see the *Congressional Record*, January 8, 2009, S181ff. For Barack Obama's remarks, "President Obama Delivers Remarks to State Department Employees," *Washington Post*, January 22, 2009.

176. Richard Falk, "Gaza: Silence Is Not an Option," United Nations Press Release, Geneva, December 9, 2008.

177. For a discussion of recent Israeli practices through the first quarter of 2008, see Edward S. Herman and David Peterson, "Principles of the Imperial New World Order," *Electric Politics*, May 1, 2008, http://www.electricpolitics.com/2008/05/principles_of_the_impe rial_new.html. For the remarks by Cardinal Renato Martino, see "Vatican deplores Gaza situation," BBC News, January 8, 2009.

178. Richard Falk, "Statement of the Special Rapporteur for the Palestinian Territories . . . ," UN Human Rights Council, Geneva, January 9, 2009; "Israel used white phosphorus in Gaza civilian areas," Amnesty International, January 19, 2009; and *Israel/Occupied Palestinian Territories: The conflict in Gaza: A briefing on applicable law, investigations and accountability*, Amnesty International, January 19, 2009.

179. "The grave violations of human rights in the Occupied Palestinian

Territory . . ." (A/HRC/S-9/L.1), UN Human Rights Council, Geneva, January 12, 2009. The vote was thirty-three in favor, one against (Canada), and thirteen abstentions.

180. For four analyses of the Israelis' wholesale slaughter of the Gaza Palestinians, see Noam Chomsky, "'Exterminate all the Brutes': Gaza 2009," *ChomskyInfo*, January 19, 2009, http://www.chomsky.info/articles/20090119.htm; Norman Finkelstein, "Behind the Bloodbath in Gaza: Foiling Another Palestinian 'Peace Initiative,'" *CounterPunch*, January 28, 2009; Henry Siegman, "Israel's Lies," *London Review of Books*, January 29, 2009; and Michael Mandel, "Self-Defense Against Peace," *CounterPunch*, February 5, 2009.

181. 2005 World Summit Outcome (A/60/L.1), UN General Assembly, September 15, 2005, http://www.who.int/hiv/universalaccess2010/worldsummit.pdf, para. 138–140.

182. "Civilians in armed conflict," First Session (S/PV.6066) and Second Session (S/PV.6066 Resumption 1), January 14, 2009. In Egyptian Ambassador Maged Abdelaziz's words: "[Egypt] believes that the Security Council has a great responsibility to impose the international will represented in its resolutions and statements . . . and provide international protection through a protection force for the Palestinian people, in implementation of the principle of the responsibility to protect. Some seek to apply that principle to specific countries, while bypassing others toiling under brutal occupation and confronting ferocious aggression without any international force to protect them" (Second Session, 31).

183. "The Georgia-Russia Crisis and the Responsibility to Protect: A Background Note," Global Center for the Responsibility to Protect, City University of New York, August 19, 2008.

184. Factiva database search carried out under both "Wires" (twir) and "Newspapers: All" (tnwp) categories for the twenty-three-day period from December 27, 2008, through January 18, 2009. Exact search parameters were: rst=(twir or tnwp) and (responsibility to protect or r2p) and gaza.

185. See Richard Goldstone *et al.*, *Human Rights in Palestine and Other Occupied Arab Territories*, Report of the United Nations Fact Finding Mission on the Gaza Conflict (A/HRC/12/48), UN Human Rights Council, September 15, 2009, http://www2.ohchr.org/english/bodies/hrcouncil/specialsession/9/docs/UNFFMGC_Report.pdf.

186. Louis Charbonneau, "U.S. doubts UN report on possible Israel war crimes," Reuters, September 17, 2009.

187. Goldstone *et al.*, *Human Rights in Palestine and Other Occupied Arab Territories*, para. 1677–1692.

188. Achim Steiner *et al.*, *Environmental Assessment of the Gaza Strip Following the Escalation of Hostilities in December 2008–January 2009*, UN Environment Program (Nairobi: United Nations Environment Programme, September 2009), 3, 55–60, 70–71, http://www.unep.org/PDF/dmb/UNEP_Gaza_EA.pdf.

189. Herb Keinon and E. B. Solomont, "PM appeals to world leaders to reject Goldstone findings," *Jerusalem Post*, September 17, 2009. Similarly, the Israeli political leadership spoke in a single voice of Israel's right and of the right of "all democracies" to defend themselves against terrorism, and of how the world "should be worried that [the Goldstone] report throws out the narrative of democracies fighting terrorists, and embraces the idea that terrorists are freedom fighters entitled to act the way they do" (the Israeli Foreign Ministry's Simona Halperin).

190. Benjamin Netanyahu, Address before the General Debate of the 64th Session of the UN General Assembly, New York, September 24, 2009.

191. Benjamin Netanyahu, *Terrorism: How the West Can Win* (New York: Farrar, Straus & Giroux, 1986), 9.

192. "Peres: Goldstone report mocks history," UPI News Tracker, September 16, 2009; Alan M. Dershowitz, "UN Investigation of Israel Discredits Itself and Undercuts Human Rights," *Huffington Post*, September 18, 2009; and Gerald M. Steinberg, "U.N. Smears Israeli Self-Defense As 'War Crimes,'" *Wall Street Journal*, September 16, 2009.

193. Goldstone *et al.*, *Human Rights in Palestine and Other Occupied Arab Territories*, para. 1766. The Commission made exactly the same recommendation with regard to the Gaza Palestinian leadership.

194. See "Why No Justice in Gaza? Israel Is Different, and so . . . ," Human Rights Watch, October 1, 2009; "UN: US Block on Goldstone Report Must Not Defer Justice," Human Rights Watch, October 2, 2009; and "UN rights body defers vote on Gaza war crime report," Reuters, October 2, 2009.

195. See, e.g., Tim Ripley, *Operation Deliberate Force: The UN and NATO Campaign in Bosnia 1995* (Lancaster: Centre for Defence and International Security Studies, 1999), 177–200, esp. the maps detailing the large, simultaneous, and clearly coordinated Croat and Bosnian Muslim offensives against the Krajina's ethnic Serb population (186–189); and Ken Silverstein, *Private Warriors* (New York: Verso, 2000), esp. chap. 4, "Mercenary, Inc.," 171–175.

196. See "The situation in the Republic of Bosnia and Herzegovina" (S/PV.3564), UN Security Council, August 10, 1995, 6–7; and "Croatia" (S/PV.3563), UN Security Council, August 10, 1995, 20.

197. See the *Judgment, Prosecutor v. Radislav Krstic* (IT-98-33-T), August 2, 2001, para. 589.

198. *Prosecutor v. Ante Gotovina et al.* (IT-06-90), June 23, 2008, 4937, lines 1–8; 4939, lines 13–14.

199. "U.S. rejects British claim of Croat ethnic cleansing," Reuters, August 8, 1995, citing Galbraith's comments over BBC Radio.

200. See Edward S. Herman, "Why the 'International Community' Does Not Deal with the Huge Dasht-e-Leili Massacre," ZNet, April 7, 2004, http://www.zmag.org/zspace/commentaries/1913.

201. Babak Dehghanpisheh *et al.*, "The Death Convoy of Afghanistan," *Newsweek*, August 26, 2002.

202. Kathy Gannon, "Group: Mass Graves in Afghanistan," Associated Press, May 1, 2002; Carlotta Gall, "Study Hints at Mass Killing of the Taliban," *New York Times*, May 1, 2002; and "Physicians for Human Rights Calls for End to Stalling of Investigation into Afghan Mass Graves," News Release, August 18, 2002.

203. "Statement by Frank Donahue, CEO, on Dasht-e-Leili Mass Grave in Afghanistan," Physicians for Human Rights, December 11, 2008; Tom Lasseter, "Mass graves still unguarded as U.S., UN, Afghans duck task," McClatchy Newspapers, December 18, 2008.

204. See James Risen, "U.S. Inaction Seen after Taliban P.O.W.s Died," *New York Times*, July 11, 2009; and "The Truth about Dasht-i-Leili," Editorial, *New York Times*, July 14, 2009.

205. See John F. Burns, "Foreign Prisoners Becoming a Problem for Karzai," *New York Times*, August 23, 2002; and John F. Burns, "Political Realities Impeding Full Inquiry into Afghan Atrocity," *New York Times*, August 29, 2002.

206. "The Truth about Dasht-i-Leili," Editorial, *New York Times*, July 14, 2009.

207. John F. Burns, "Political Realities Impeding Full Inquiry Into Afghan Atrocity," *New York Times*, August 29, 2002. "Shibarghan" refers to a prison in northern Afghanistan to and from which the captured enemies of the U.S.-led forces were transported in airtight shipping containers in which several thousand are believed to have died.

208. See the entries for Turkey in the annual Human Rights Watch *World Reports* dating back as far as HRW's electronic archives run, http://www.hrw.org/en/node/79288.

209. See, e.g., John Tirman, *Spoils of War: The Human Cost of America's Arms Trade* (New York: The Free Press, 1997), chap. 23, "The Terrible Reckoning," 254–278. We differ with Tirman in this respect: That we believe the U.S. policymaking elite is second to none in regarding military aid (arms sales, training, "interoperability") as the "fulcrum, the sine qua non," of the U.S. link to foreign governments.

Indeed, it is hardly an afterthought when the "arrival of shiny high-tech weapons, the conveyance of case, the primary of military-to-military lines in the bilateral relationship—all bolster the military elites, enabling them to exert more political power, draw on more national resources, and, of course, shape national policy." Washington gets what it pays for. (Cf. chap. 24, "The Moral Equation," 279–287.)

210. Edward S. Herman and Noam Chomsky, *Manufacturing Consent: The Political Economy of the Mass Media* (New York: Pantheon, 2002), xxi.

211. Factiva database searches carried out under the "Wires" (*twir*) and "Newspapers: All" (*tnwp*) categories for the years 1984–2008; searches performed on January 26, 2009. We used the database operators w/5 and * to capture all variations of words occurring anywhere within five words of the other primary search terms; and we used the limiter not to exclude all items that also mentioned any one or more of the other search terms. The exact search parameters were:

(1) rst=(twir or tnwp) and Turkey and (**Kurd*** w/5 genocid*) not (Afghanistan or Bosnia or Burundi or Cambodia or Congo or Darfur or East Timor or Ethiopia or Guatemala or Indonesia or Iraq or Kosovo or Rwanda or Sudan or Vietnam or Armen*) : 20

(2) rst=(twir or tnwp) and Turkey and (**Armen*** w/5 genocid*) not (Afghanistan or Bosnia or Burundi or Cambodia or Congo or Darfur or East Timor or Ethiopia or Guatemala or Indonesia or Iraq or Kosovo or Rwanda or Sudan or Vietnam or Kurd*) : 9,627

(3) rst=(twir or tnwp) and Iraq and (**Kurd*** w/5 genocid*) not (Afghanistan or Bosnia or Burundi or Cambodia or Congo or Darfur or East Timor or Ethiopia or Guatemala or Indonesia or Kosovo or Rwanda or Sudan or Turkey or Vietnam or Armen*) : 296

212. John Pilger, "Land of the Dead," *The Nation*, April 25, 1994.

213. Daniel Patrick Moynihan and Suzanne Weaver, *A Dangerous Place* (New York: Little Brown, 1978), 247.

214. See Chomsky and Herman, *The Washington Connection and Third World Fascism*, Sect. 3.4.4, "East Timor: Genocide on the Sly," 129–204.

215. Henry Kamm, "The Silent Suffering of East Timor," *New York Times Magazine*, February 15, 1981; Henry Kamm, "Post-Colonial Oppressors," *New York Times Book Review*, January 11, 1987.

216. See Edward S. Herman and David Peterson, "How the *New York Times* Protects Indonesia Terror in East Timor," *Z Magazine*, July, 1999, http://www.zmag.org/zmag/viewArticle/13140; and "East Timor: From Humanitarian Bombing to Inhumane Appeasement," *Covert Action Quarterly*, Fall/Winter 1999, No. 68, http://covertaction.org/ content/view/65/75.

217. See Richard Lloyd Parry, "Timor's fear of Jakarta troops," *The Independent*, October 9, 1998; Richard Lloyd Parry, "Troops sent in despite promises," *The Independent*, October 24, 1998; and Richard Lloyd Parry, "Timor military retreat 'a sham,'" *The Independent*, October 30, 1998.

218. Allan Nairn, "License to Kill in Timor," *The Nation*, May 31, 1999.

219. See "Unlawful Killings and Enforced Disappearances," para. 774–778, a section of chap. 2 of the larger *Chega! Report of the Commission for Reception, Truth and Reconciliation in East Timor*, International Center for Transitional Justice, January 30, 2006, http://www.ictj.org/en/news/features/846.html. For the higher estimates, see Lindsay Murdoch, "Horror Lives On for Town of Liquiçá," *Sydney Morning Herald*, April 8, 2000; and Barry Wain, "Will Justice Be Served in East Timor?" *Wall Street Journal*, April 14, 2000.

220. Allan Nairn, "U.S. Complicity in Timor," *The Nation*, September 27, 1999.

221. Jose Ramos-Horta, "Yes to Kosovo, No to East Timor?" *International Herald Tribune*, April 29, 1999.

222. Belisario Betancur et al., *From Madness to Hope: The 12-Year War in El Salvador. Report of the Commission for Truth of El Salvador*, March 1993, Part IV, "Cases and Patterns of Violence," Section C, "Massacres of Peasants by Armed Forces," specifically "El Mozote 1981," http://www.usip.org/library/tc/doc/reports/el_salvador/tc_es_03151993_toc.html%20.

223. Christian Tomuschat et al., *Guatemala: Memory of Silence: Report of the Commission for Historical Clarification* (Guatemalan Commission for Historical Clarification, February 1999), specifically the "Conclusions," para. 86, and "Map: Number of Massacres by Department," http://shr.aaas.org/guatemala/ceh/report/english/toc.html.

224. Herman and Chomsky, *Manufacturing Consent*, chap. 3, "Legitimizing versus meaningless Third World Elections: El Salvador, Guatemala, and Nicaragua," 87–142. The authors conclude with the "tentative generalization that the U.S. mass media will always find a Third World election sponsored by their own government a 'step toward democracy', and an election held in a country that their government is busily destabilizing a farce and a sham"—in short, "what a propaganda model would predict" (141).

225. See Raymond Bonner, *Weakness and Deceit: U.S. Policy and El Salvador* (New York: Times Books, 1984).

226. "[T]he vaunted Col. Domingo Monterrosa ordered the attack in El Mozote, which [former Salvadoran soldier] Salgada said he now con-

siders 'a genocide.'" (*Washington Post*, January 29, 2007.)

227. Tomuschat, *Guatemala: Memory of Silence*, specifically "Conclusions," para. 120, 122.

228. Herman and Chomsky, *Manufacturing Consent*, ch. 2, "Worthy and Unworthy Victims," 37–86; esp. 71–79.

229. AP, "Mutilated Bodies Found after Serb Attack," *New York Times*, January 17, 1999; Juliet Terzieff, "Kosovo Serbs massacre 45 villagers," *Sunday Times* (U.K.), January 17, 1999; Guy Dinmore, "Villagers Slaughtered in Kosovo 'Atrocity,'" *Washington Post*, January 17, 1999.

230. Barton Gellman, "The Path to Crisis: How the United States and Its Allies Went to War," *Washington Post*, April 18, 1999.

231. The Kosovo Verification Mission was created by the agreement between Belgrade and NATO special representative Richard Holbrooke in October 1998, and called for up to 2,000 unarmed monitors to operate inside Kosovo to verify Serbian compliance with a cease-fire and partial withdrawal of Serbian troops from the province. But as a Swiss member of the mission later told the Swiss journal *La Liberté*: "We understood from the start that information gathered by OSCE patrols during our missions was destined to complete the information that NATO had gathered by satellite. We had the very sharp impression of doing espionage work for the Atlantic Alliance." See Diana Johnstone, "Humanitarian War: Making the Crime Fit the Punishment," in Tariq Ali, ed., *Masters of the Universe: NATO's Balkans Crusade* (New York: Verso, 2000), 162.

232. According to Michael Mandel, William Walker's "unsavory missions" in the 1980s included activities to overthrow the Sandinista government of Nicaragua that led to his being a "'subject of investigation' in the Iran/Contra Affair for his involvement with Oliver North. . . ." (*How America Gets Away with Murder*, 77, and n. 98, 267.)

233. Lee Hockstader, "Our Man in El Salvador," *Washington Post*, December 19, 1989; Elizabeth Shogren, "William Walker, once criticized for his inaction in El Salvador, is treated like a hero by ethnic Albanian refugees," *Los Angeles Times*, April 14, 1999.

234. See our treatment of the "Račak Massacre" in Edward S. Herman and David Peterson, "CNN: Selling NATO's War Globally," in Hammond and Herman, *Degraded Capability*, 111–122, esp. 117–119. (Also posted at http://www.zcommunications.org/cnn-selling-natos-war-globally-by-david-peterson.)

235. This account draws in part on the personal statement issued by the Finnish pathologist Helena Ranta on March 17, 1999, in conjunction with the release of the Report of the EU Forensic Team on the Račak Incident. Ranta participated in the Team's work in performing the

autopsies. Her statement appears in Marc Weller, ed., *The Crisis in Kosovo 1989–1999* (Cambridge, U.K.: Documents & Analysis Publishing, Ltd., 1999), 333–335.

236. "Forty-five slain in Kosovo massacre," Agence France Presse, January 16, 1999. A flattering profile of William Walker on ABC–TV's *Nightline* called him a "Man with a Mission" (January 29, 1999).

237. Marc Weller, *The Crisis in Kosovo 1989–1999*, 291.

238. "Forensic expert says she was told to blame Serbs for Račak killings," Agence France Presse, October 22, 2008. The biography reported here is by Kaius Niemi, and titled "Helena Ranta, Human Mark."

239. Mandel, *How America Gets Away with Murder*, 73.

240. See J. Rainio *et al.*, "Independent forensic autopsies in an armed conflict: investigation of the victims from Račak, Kosovo," *Forensic Science International*, Vol. 116, No. 2, 2001, 171–185, http://www.journals.elsevierhealth.com/periodicals/fsi/article/PIIS0379073800003923/abstract.

241. *Ibid.*, Table 3, Principal Findings, 179.

242. Rainio *et al.* clearly distinguish between cause of death (i.e., in the present cases, gunshot wounds) and manner of death, i.e., combatant versus noncombatant, or deaths occurring in battle and execution-style deaths. Only execution-style death qualifies for inclusion in the "massacre" model.

243. *Ibid.*, 180, 183.

244. For some additional sources, see "Forensic Institute Says No Evidence Kosovo Albanians Massacred," BBC Summary of World Broadcasts, February 18, 1999; "Prosecutor Says No Reason to Charge Police Involved in Attack in Kosovo," BBC Summary of World Broadcasts, March 12, 1999; "Finnish autopsies on Račak massacre are inconclusive: report," Agence France Presse, March 17, 1999; and "Yugoslav Forensic Experts Say 'No Massacre' in Kosovo," BBC Summary of World Broadcasts, March 18, 1999; and Julius Strauss, "Kosovo killings inquiry verdict sparks outrage," *Daily Telegraph*, March 18, 1999.

245. "Clinton Voices Anger and Compassion at Serbian Intransigence on Kosovo," *New York Times*, March 20, 1999.

246. *Prosecutor Against Slobodan Milosevic et al.* (IT-99-37), May 22, 1999. See Schedule A: "Persons Known by Name Killed at Račak—15 January 1999." The very next incident covered by the Initial Indictment for Kosovo, listed in Schedule B, occurred at Bela Crkva, and was dated March 25, 1999—one day after NATO launched Operation Allied Force on March 24.

247. Holding our media universe constant for the nineteen-year period

from 1990 through 2008, we find that in 1990 forms of the word "genocide" appeared in 1,352 different items. But by 1999, usage of the word had increased by 252% (4,758 items), and by 2006, the high-water mark for "genocide" usage through 2008, it had increased by 297% (5,369 items). Factiva database searches on a year-by-year basis, using the parameters: *rst=(nytf or j or wp or usat or atjc or bstngb or sfc or dal or grdn or ob or ind or indos or t or st or ec or smhh or glob or tor or lba) and genocid**.

248. Herman and Chomsky, *Manufacturing Consent*, xxi.

249. A search of the UN News Center's database for reports that mentioned Darfur and reports that mentioned Iraq during the five year period from 2004 through 2008 found that whereas Darfur was mentioned in 1,711 different UN News Center reports, Iraq was mentioned in 1,555—10% fewer than Darfur. In short, the UN's subservience to the United States succeeded in channeling its attention toward Darfur, crowding out the conflicts and crises caused by the U.S. war and occupation of a sovereign country, in unambiguous violation of both the letter and the spirit of the United Nations' primary reason for being.

250. Luis Moreno-Ocampo, *Prosecutor's Statement on the Prosecutor's Application for a Warrant of Arrest under Article 58 Against Omar Hassan Ahmad Al Bashir*, International Criminal Court, The Hague, 2, http://www.icc-cpi.int/library/organs/otp/ICC-OTP-ST200807 14-ENG.pdf; also see the accompanying Press Release, July 14, 2008, http://www.icc-cpi.int/press/pressreleases/406.html.

251. For example: "[T]he clearest assertion that in the 21st century, mass murder is no longer a ruler's prerogative" (Nicholas D. Kristof, *New York Times*, February 26, 2009); "[A]n important declaration to the world that no person, no matter how powerful, is immune from the reach of justice in the 21st century" (Lloyd Axworthy, former Foreign Minister of Canada, *Toronto Globe and Mail*, March 4, 2009); "Not even presidents are guaranteed a free pass for horrific crimes" (Richard Dicker, International Justice Program Director, Human Rights Watch, March 4, 2009); "This announcement is an important signal—both for Darfur and the rest of the world—that suspected human rights violators will face trial, no matter how powerful they are" (Irene Khan, Secretary General, Amnesty International, March 4, 2009); "[I]t tells the 300,000 brutally killed and 2.5 million displaced and raped and maimed that justice must always prevail. That the rest of the world sees their struggle and stands up and demands justice" (George Clooney, Hollywood actor and UN Messenger for Peace, *The Daily Beast*, March 4, 2009); "[T]he message for tyrants the

world over must be that they cannot evade justice forever" (*The Times of London*, March 5, 2009); "There can be no impunity for such atrocities.... Any country that continues to enable Mr. Bashir should be branded as an accomplice to his many horrors" (*New York Times*, March 7, 2009).

252. See Tsegaye Tadesse, "ICC genocide charge sought for Sudan's Bashir," Reuters, July 7, 2009. On July 3, citing its unhappiness with the UN Security Council's refusal "to defer the proceedings against al-Bashir," the African Union issued a declaration stating that "the AU Member States shall not cooperate pursuant to the provisions of Article 98 of the Rome Statute of the ICC relating to immunities, for the arrest and surrender of President Bashir." Coming only four days later, Moreno-Ocampo's call for the ICC to re-hear his evidence for the "genocide" count against al-Bashir showed the politicization of the ICC once again.

253. Judge Akua Kuenyehia *et al.*, *The Case of the Prosecutor v. Omar Hassan Ahmad Al Bashir* (ICC-02/05-01/09), International Criminal Court, The Hague, March 4, 2009, para. 40, 42, http://www.icc-cpi.int/iccdocs/doc/doc639096.pdf.

254. "[T]he Chamber observes that, . . . article 27(1) and (2) of the [Rome] Statute provide for the following core principles: (i) 'This Statute shall apply equally to all persons without any distinction based on official capacity'; (ii) '...official capacity...shall in no case exempt a person from criminal responsibility under this Statute . . .'." *Ibid.*, para. 43.

255. Kofi Annan, "Statement by the United Nations Secretary-General Kofi Annan," July 18, 1998.

256. See the Rome Statute, http://untreaty.un.org/cod/icc/index.html.

257. See the website of the Special Working Group on the Crime of Aggression, ICC, http://www.icc-cpi.int/Menus/ASP/Crime+of+Aggression. Through 2009, the plans were to base the ICC's definition of aggression on the UN General Assembly's definition of December 14, 1974 (A/RES/3314—see the Annex). In brief, while excluding acts of terrorism carried out by non-state actors, the proposed definition would include "invasion, attacking another State, or the military occupation of another State, however temporary," as well as "bombardments against another State, carrying out blockades, allowing another State to perpetrate acts of aggression against a third State, or sending armed bands to carry out grave acts against other States." See "Press Conference on Special Working Group on Crime of Aggression," UN Department of Public Information, February 13, 2009,

http://www.un.org/News/briefings/docs/2009/090213_ICC.doc. htm. However, we strongly suspect that this Working Group's mission will remain unfulfilled. Or, even if it were to succeed, the new prohibition would be implemented in as selective and discriminatory a fashion as are the rest of the Rome Statute's laws today.

258. Michael Mandel, *How America Gets Away with Murder*, 207–208.

259. *Ibid.*, 208–209. The phrase "standing tribunal that could be activated immediately" derives from David J. Scheffer, the Clinton administration's Ambassador-at-Large for War Crimes and the chief U.S. negotiator at the Rome Conference, "The United States and the International Criminal Court," *American Journal of International Law*, Vol. 93, 1999.

260. See UN Security Council Resolution 1593 (S/RES/1593), March 31, 2005.

261. See "State Parties to the Rome Statute," International Criminal Court, http://www.icc-cpi.int/statesparties.html. Other noteworthy non-State Parties as of mid-2009 included China, Russia, India, Israel, Iran, Pakistan, Rwanda, and the Sudan—the Sudan's case only having been placed under the ICC's jurisdiction through a referral by the Security Council.

262. Luis Moreno-Ocampo, Chief Prosecutor of the International Criminal Court, Correspondence dated February 9, 2006, http://www.icc-cpi.int/library/organs/otp/OTP_letter_to_ senders_re_Iraq_9_February_2006.pdf.

263. See *Final Report to the Prosecutor by the Committee Established to Review the NATO Bombing Campaign Against the Federal Republic of Yugoslavia*, Office of the Prosecutor, ICTY, June, 2000, para. 90, http://www.un.org/icty/pressreal/nato061300.htm.

264. See Louise Arbour, *Prosecutor of the Tribunal Against Slobodan Milosevic et al.* (IT-99-37), Schedules A–G, May 22, 1999, http://www.un.org/ icty/indictment/english/mil-ii990524e.htm. These schedules list the names of 344 dead Kosovo Albanians whom, in this particular case, constituted a sufficient "crime base" to bring the indictment. As noted, however, the deaths of only the forty-five persons named in Schedule A ("Račak," January 15, 1999) date from prior to the start of NATO's war. As we point out in our text, the "Račak Massacre" is almost surely mythical.

265. "Press Conference Given by NATO Spokesman Jamie Shea, and SHAPE Spokesman, Major General Walter Jertz," NATO HQ, Brussels, May 17, 1999, http://www.nato.int/kosovo/press/p990517b.htm.

266. Conservative estimates of the number of Ugandans killed under the Idi Amin dictatorship (1971–1979) are 100,000 victims, with high-

end estimates of some 300,000. See Richard H. Ulmann, "Human Rights and Economic Power: The United States versus Idi Amin," *Foreign Affairs*, April 1978. As Ulmann noted at the time, "In any contemporary lexicon of horror, Uganda is synonymous with state-become-slaughterhouse." This is manifestly not true of Rwanda or the Democratic Republic of Congo in the areas under Kagame-RPF control: No matter how many lives Kagame and the RFP have taken, and these number many times the Idi Amin toll, their reign of terror has never entered the contemporary lexicon of horror.

267. See the verbatim record of the oral arguments by the U.S. legal representatives, *Request for the indication of provisional measures, Yugoslavia v. United States of America*, ICJ, 4:30 PM, May 12, 1999, para. 2.1–2.24, here para. 2.22, http://www.icj-cij.org/docket/files/114/4577.pdf.

268. See *Yugoslavia v. United States of America*, June 2, 1999, para. 26–34, http://www.icj-cij.org/docket/files/114/8036.pdf. Each of the other nine cases (i.e., against Belgium, Canada, France, Germany, Italy, the Netherlands, Portugal, Spain, and the United Kingdom) turned out the same.

269. See the press release, "ICC issues a warrant of arrest for Omar Al Bashir, President of Sudan" (ICC-CPI-20090304-PR394), International Criminal Court, The Hague, March 4, 2009.

270. We are referring to Samantha Power's 2002 *"A Problem from Hell": America and the Age of Genocide*, awarded the 2003 Pulitzer Prize in the General Nonfiction category.

Index

Abdelaziz, Maged, 76
Abdullah, Youssef Yakob, 41
Adams, John Quincy, 8
Afghanistan: Dasht-e-Leili in,
    84–86; Obama administration
    in, 116–17n27
aggression, as crime, 21; attempts
    to define, 148–49n257; Rome
    Statute on, 106
Agwai, Martin, 44–45
Al-Anfal campaign (Iraq), 87
Albanians: in Kosovo, 49, 50, 74,
    127–28n99; Račak massacre of,
    95, 96
Albright, Madeleine K., 32, 82, 96,
    115n18
Allawi, Ayad, 36–37
Amanpour, Christiane, 19, 20
America: colonial history of, 9–10.
    See also United States
Amin, Idi, 110, 150n266
Amnesty International: on aggres-
    sion, 21; on Guatemala, 93, 94
Annan, Kofi, 40, 61, 95, 105–6
Arabs: in Darfur Wars, 41–42, 45

Arafat, Yasir, 71
Arbenz, Jacobo, 15, 92
Arbour, Louise, 59, 95–96, 99–100,
    109
Armed Forces of Rwanda (FAR),
    58, 59
Armenian genocide, 88
Arusha Peace Accords (1993), 54,
    55
Australia, 26
Axworthy, Lloyd, 147–48n251

Bagosora, Théoneste, 130n115
Baker, Russell, 8–9
al-Bashir, Omar Hassan Ahmad:
    indictment of, 104–5, 107,
    116n21, 147–48n251
Beirut (Lebanon), 70–71
benign genocides, 104; in
    Afghanistan, 84–86; in Central
    America, 91–94; in Croatia,
    81–83; definition of, 16; in East
    Timor, 89–91; in El Salvador,
    91–92; in Gaza Strip, 73–81;
    against Kurds, 87–88; in

Lebanon, by Israel, 69–71
Biden, Joseph, 12; on Iraq, 37–38
Binder, David, 127–28n99
blacks: in Darfur, 41–42, 45
Blair, Dennis, 90
bloodbaths: categories of, 16, 104.
    See also genocide
Bonner, Raymond, 92
Bosnia and Herzegovina, 46–48;
    Croatia and, 82; media refer-
    ences to genocide in, 33
Boutros-Ghali, Boutros, 63–64,
    135n148
Bricmont, Jean, 25
Britain. See United Kingdom
Bruguière, Jean-Louis, 60–61
Burns, John, 86
Burundi, 16, 57, 60
Bush, George W.: Afghanistan war
    under, 116–17n27; on pre-emp-
    tive self defense, 21
Bush (G.W.B.) administration:
    Dasht-e-Leili and, 85–86
Bush Doctrine, 8

Cambodia, 16, 18, 20, 103–4
Carter, Jimmy, 89
Central America, 91–94
Chatelet, Christophe, 97, 98
Chávez, Hugo, 81
children: in Iraq, under sanctions,
    31, 32
China: Sudan and, 39
Chomsky, Noam, 7–12; Counter-
    Revolutionary Violence:
    Bloodbaths in Fact and
    Propaganda by, 15–17; on
    Kahan Commission, 138n166;
    on Kosovo, 127–28n99; on
    "Responsibility to Protect," 25,
    27

Christian Phalange (Lebanon),
    70–71
Christian Science Monitor, 81
Christopher, Warren, 57
civilian populations: in Gaza Strip,
    75, 77; Geneva Conventions on,
    118–19n39; during Iraqi inva-
    sion and occupation, 34–37;
    during Iraqi sanctions, 30–32
climate change: as issue in Darfur,
    41
Clinton, Bill, 20, 95, 99, 100
Clinton, Hillary, 75
Clooney, George, 147–48n251
Cohen, Herman, 53, 64
Cohen, Roger, 10
Cohen, William S., 50, 115n18
Columbus, Christopher, 8–9
Congo, Democratic Republic of:
    death toll in, 43–44; invaded by
    Uganda, 66–67; media refer-
    ences to genocide in, 33; S. Rice
    on genocide in, 23–24; United
    Nations on, 67–68
conquistadors, 9
constructive genocides, 103; defini-
    tion of, 16; during Iraqi invasion
    and occupation, 33–38; during
    Iraqi sanctions, 29–33
Cook, Robin, 95
Corfu Channel case (World
    Court), 10
Counter-Revolutionary Violence:
    Bloodbaths in Fact and
    Propaganda (Chomsky and
    Herman), 15–17
Croatia, 81–83

Darfur (Sudan), 39–45; arrest war-
    rant for, 104–5; media refer-
    ences to genocide in, 33; S. Rice

on genocide in, 23; United Nations Security Council on, 107

Dasht-e-Leili (Afghanistan), 84–86

Davenport, Christian, 58–59, 132–33n129

Del Ponte, Carla, 61–62, 109

Dershowitz, Alan, 79

Des Forges, Alison, 51–52, 65, 129–30n109

de Waal, Alex, 45

Dicker, Richard, 147–48n251

Diem, Ngo Dinh, 19

Doran, Jamie, 84, 85

Dostum, 86

Dugard, John, 74, 79

Dunjic, Dusan, 98

East Pakistan, 16

East Timor, 20; invaded by Indonesia, 64; Liquiçá in, 89–91; Power on, 17–18; Timor Gap Oil Treaty on, 26

Egeland, Jan, 136n158

Eisenhower, Dwight D., 13

Eitan, Raphael, 70, 71

elections, 92, 144n224

Ellis, John, 22

El Mozote (El Salvador), 92, 94, 100–101

El Quiche (Guatemala), 93

El Salvador, 91–92, 96–97

England. See United Kingdom

Enough Project, 45

environmental issues: in Darfur, 41; in Gaza Strip, 77–78

Escoto Brockmann, Miguel d', 25

ethnic cleansing, 78; in Bosnia and Herzegovina, 46, 47; in Croatia, 82, 83; in Darfur, 40; "Responsibility to Protect" from,

20, 22, 26; in Rwanda, 53, 57, 63

Evans, Gareth, 25–27, 118n36

Fact Finding Mission on the Gaza Conflict (UN; Goldstone Commission), 77–80

Fake, Steven, 44

Falk, Richard, 11, 34, 75, 79

Fallujah (Iraq), 37

FAR. See Armed Forces of Rwanda

Florida, 8

France: Rwanda and, 60, 129–30n109

Fretilin (East Timor), 89

Friel, Howard, 34

Funk, Kevin, 44

Gaddis, John Lewis, 8

Galbraith, Peter, 83

Gaza Strip, 73–81

Gemayel, Bashir, 70

Geneva Conventions: Iraqi sanctions and, 30; Israel under, 79; on protection of civilian populations, 118–19n39

genocide: Armenian genocide, 88; in Bosnia and Herzegovina, 47–48; categories of, 16; in Kosovo, 50–51; in Rwanda, 51–53; United States policy on, 23–24

genocide, media references to: in Central America, 92, 94; in Darfur, 39; in East Timor, 89; in Gaza Strip, 80–81; increase in, 103; in Iraq, 38, 122–23n62; during Iraqi sanctions, 32–33; in Kosovo, 51; on Kurds, 88; in Lebanon, 71

Genocide Prevention Task Force, 19; on Darfur, 43

Gersony, Robert, 57, 59
Global Center for the
    Responsibility to Protect (City
    University of New York), 76–77
Goldstone, Richard, 59–60, 77–79
Goldstone Commission (UN Fact
    Finding Mission on the Gaza
    Conflict), 77–80
Gourevitch, Philip, 62–63, 110
Great Britain. *See* United Kingdom
Guatemala, 91–94; Arbenz over-
    thrown in, 15
Guernica (Spain), 37

Habyarimana, Juvénal, 51–56;
    assassination of, 59–60, 62,
    134n141; human rights organi-
    zations on, 65, 66
Hakizimana, Christophe, 132n127
Halabja massacre (Iraq), 87–88
Halliday, Denis, 30
Hamas (Gaza Strip), 74, 75
Hartmann, Florence, 62
Herold, Marc W., 116–17n27
Herzegovina. *See* Bosnia and
    Herzegovina
Hezbollah, 81
Hodgson, Geoffrey, 10
Holbrooke, Richard, 145n231
Holocaust, 7
Hourigan, Michael, 59, 60
human rights organizations, 64–66
Human Rights Watch (HRW): on
    aggression, 21; on Dasht-e-Leili,
    84; on Rwanda, 51, 64–66
Hussein, Saddam, 38; Kurds under,
    87–88; during sanctions against
    Iraq, 32
Hutus: massacres of, 57–58, 62, 67;
    in Rwanda, 51–53, 56, 66

Indonesia, 16–20, 115n18; East
    Timor invaded by, 64, 89–91; in
    Timor Gap Oil Treaty, 26
International Coalition for the
    Responsibility to Protect: on
    invasion of Iraq, 24
International Commission of
    Inquiry into Human Rights
    Abuses in Rwanda, 65
International Commission of
    Inquiry on Darfur, 41
International Court of Justice
    (ICJ), 110
International Criminal Court
    (ICC), 20–21, 80, 111; on
    aggression, as crime, 106–7,
    148–49n257; al-Bashir indicted
    by, 104–5; on war crimes in
    Iraq, 107–9
International Criminal Tribunal for
    Rwanda (ICTR), 21, 52, 58–62;
    verdict of, 54–55
International Criminal Tribunal for
    the Former Yugoslavia (ICTY),
    21, 46; on Kosovo, 49; on
    Krstic, 47; Milosevic indicted
    by, 109–10; on Operation
    Storm, 82–83
International Federation of Human
    Rights, 51
international law: on invasion and
    occupation of Iraq, 34, 37; Israel
    under, 79; NATO under, 109;
    on protection of civilian popula-
    tions, 118–19n39; Rome
    Statute, 105–6; United States
    under, 110–11
International Security Assistance
    Force (Afghanistan), 85
Iran: Mosaddeq overthrown in, 15;
    threatened by Israel, 12

Iraq, 104; current U.S. policy on, 24–25; Evans on invasion of, 118*n*36; invasion and occupation of, 33–38; investigation of war crimes in, 107–9; Kurds in, 87–88; sanctions against, 29–33

Islam. *See* Muslims

Israel: Gaza Strip invaded by, 73–81; Iran threatened by, 12; Lebanon invaded by, 69–72

Israel Defense Force (IDF): in Gaza Strip, 73–74; in Lebanon, 70–71

Izetbegovic, Alija, 125*n*88

Jacoby, Daniel, 65–66

Jallow, Hassan, 62, 134*n*141

Kabila, Joseph, 67

Kabila, Laurent, 67

Kabiligi, Gratien, 130*n*115

Kagame, Paul, 20, 23, 53, 59, 66, 105, 110; Del Ponte and, 61; Gourevitch on, 135*n*143; Habyarimana's assassination and, 60; Kinzer on, 135*n*144; U.S. support for, 55–56, 62–63, 68

Kahan Commission of Inquiry (Israel), 71, 137*n*163

Kamm, Henry, 89–90

Kapeliouk, Amnon, 70, 71

Kapila, Mukesh, 40

Karzai, Hamid, 86

Keep the Promise: Sudan Now (organization), 45

Kennan, George, 13, 15

Khan, Irene, 147–48*n*251

Ki-moon, Ban, 41; on invasion of Gaza Strip, 74

Kinzer, Stephen, 63

Knox, Henry, 7–8

Kosovo, 46, 49–51; Albanians in, 74; media references to genocide in, 33; Račak massacre in, 27, 91, 95–101

Kosovo Liberation Army (KLA), 49–50, 97, 100, 127–28*n*99

Kosovo Verification Mission, 96, 145*n*231

Krajina (Croatia), 82–83

Kristof, Nicholas, 40–41, 147–48*n*251

Krstic, Radislav, 47

Kurdish Regional Government (Iraq), 37

Kurdistan: during Iraqi sanctions, 31

Kurds, 87–88

Kuwait: Iraqi invasion of, 29

Laos, 20

Latin America, 91–94

Lebanon, 69–72, 80

Liechty, C. Philip, 89

Liquiçá (East Timor), 89–91

London Times, 95

Lord's Resistance Army (Uganda), 23

Los Angeles Times, 97

al-Maliki, Nouri, 37

Mamdani, Mahmood, 40–41

Mandel, Michael, 47, 106, 145*n*232

Massachusetts Bay Colony, 10

massacre: use of word, 100–101. *See also* bloodbaths; genocide

Mayans, 92–94

McGovern, Ray, 121*n*50

media: on Darfur Wars, 39, 43, 124*n*74; on genocide in Iraq, 38, 122–23*n*62; on impact of Iraqi

invasion on civilian population,
34; during lead-up to Iraq inva-
sion, 33, 120n48; on Račak mas-
sacre, 95, 100; use of "genocide"
by, 32–33. See also genocide,
media references to
mercenaries, 82
Milosevic, Slobodan, 100, 109–10
Mobutu, 67
Moreno-Ocampo, Luis, 104–5,
107–9
Morgan, Edmund, 8–9
Morgenthau, Hans, 10
Mosaddeq, Mohammad, 15
Moynihan, Daniel Patrick, 89
MPRI (Military Professional
Resources Inc.), 82
Mueller, John, 31
Mueller, Karl, 31
Museveni, Yoweri, 20, 23, 53, 66,
105; U.S. support for, 68
Muslims: in Bosnia, 47, 48; in
Darfur, 41; Palestinians, 70–71
My Lai massacre, 19
mythical genocides: definition of,
16; Račak, 95–101

Nagy, Thomas, 30
Nairn, Allan, 90
Native Americans (American
Indians), 8–10
Ndadaye, Melchior, 60
nefarious genocides, 103–4; in
Bosnia and Herzegovina, 46–48;
Darfur Wars, 39–45; definition
of, 16; in Kosovo, 49–51; in
Rwanda, 51–66
Neier, Aryeh, 19
Netanyahu, Benjamin, 78–79
New York Times: on Dasht-e-Leili,
85–86; on El Salvador, 92; on

Gaza Strip, 81; on Guatemala,
94; on Indonesian invasion of
East Timor, 89–90; on invasion
of Iraq, 34; during lead-up to
Iraq invasion, 120n48; on Račak
massacre, 95
Ngo Dinh Diem, 19
Nicaragua, 145n232
Nindiliyimana, Augustin, 132n127
North, Oliver, 145n232
North Atlantic Treaty Organization
(NATO): in Bosnia and
Herzegovina, 46; in Kosovo, 49,
50; Kosovo Verification Mission
of, 145n231; Račak massacre
and, 96; war crimes committed
by, 109
Northern Alliance (Afghanistan),
84
Nsengiyumva, Anatole, 130n115
Ntabakuze, Aloys, 130n115
Ntaryamira, Cyprien, 54
Nuremberg Judgment: on aggres-
sion as crime, 21; on "supreme
international crime," 34, 121n50

Obama, Barack: Afghanistan war
under, 116–17n27; on Israel,
139n175
Obama administration: on Iraq, 37;
U. S. rejoins United Nations
Human Rights Council under,
74
oil: in Iraq, during occupation, 37
Operation Flash (Western
Slavonia), 82
Operation Storm (Krajina,
Croatia), 82–83
Organization for Security and
Cooperation in Europe
(OSCE), 96, 97

Pace, Peter, 86
Palestinians: in Gaza, 73–81; in
    Sabra and Shatila, 70–71
Peres, Shimon, 78
Phalange (Lebanon), 70–71
Philippines, 15
Philpot, Robin, 65, 135n148
Physicians for Human Rights
    (PHR), 84–85
Pilger, John, 89
Popieluszko, Jerzy, 94
Porter, Michael, 20
Posner, Michael, 80
Powell, Colin, 37
Power, Samantha: on Darfur, 39;
    on Guatemala, 93; on
    Indonesian invasion of East
    Timor, 17–18; Pulitzer Prize
    won by, 111, 150n270; on
    Rwanda, 63
Prendergast, John, 43, 45
Prentice, Eve-Ann, 127–28n99
Preventing Genocide: A Blueprint for
    U.S. Policymakers (Albright and
    Cohen), 19, 115n18
Problem from Hell: America and the
    Age of Genocide, A (Power),
    17–18
Prosper, Pierre, 61

Račak (Kosovo), 91, 95–101;
    Evans on, 27
Ramos-Horta, Jose, 91
Ranta, Helena, 98, 100,
    145–46n235
Reagan, Ronald, 10
Reeves, Eric, 40
Reid, Harry, 75
Rentjens, Filip, 67, 136n157
"Responsibility to Protect" (R2P):
    Evans on, 26–27, 118n36; Gaza

Palestinians and, 76–77; S. Rice
    on, 9, 23–24; United Nations
    on, 115–16n19; in U.S. policy,
    11–12, 24–25
Rice, Susan E., 9, 10, 12; on
    Goldstone Commission, 77, 80;
    on "Responsibility to Protect,"
    23–25; on United Nations
    Human Rights Council, 74,
    139n174
Rio Negro (Guatemala), 93–94
Robertson, Geoffrey, 19
Robertson, George, 49
Robson, Eleanor, 36
Rome Statute (1998), 105–6
Roosevelt, Theodore, 10
Roth, Kenneth, 129–30n109
Rwanda, 20, 51–66; human rights
    organizations on, 64–66; inter-
    national tribunals for, 21;
    invaded by Uganda, 53–54;
    investigations into genocide in,
    59–62; media references to
    genocide in, 33; power struggle
    in, 54–55
Rwandan Patriotic Front (RPF),
    52–55, 64; human rights organi-
    zations and, 64–66; Hutus killed
    by, 57–59; investigations of,
    59–62; Rentjens on, 67; U.S.
    support for, 55–56

Sabra (Lebanon), 70–72
Sarnoff, William, 114n11
Schabas, William, 65
Scharping, Rudolf, 50
Scheffer, David J., 149n259
Schmidt, Eric, 20
Serbs, 73; in Bosnia and
    Herzegovina, 46, 48; in Croatia,
    82–83; in Kosovo, 49–50, 74,

127–28n99; Račak massacre
and, 97–99
Sharon, Ariel, 71
Shatila (Lebanon), 70–72
Shea, Jamie, 50, 109
slave trade, 22
Solana, Javier, 95
Spain: conquistadors from, 9
Sray, John, 46
Srebrenica massacre, 47–48, 82
Stahl, Lesley, 32
Stam, Allan, 55–56, 58–59,
132–33n129
Steinberg, Gerald, 79
Sudan: Darfur Wars in, 39–45;
indictment of president of,
104–5, 147–48n251; United
Nations on, 116n21. See also
Darfur
Sudan Liberation Movement, 39–40
Suharto, 89
"supreme international crime," 30,
121n50; in Rwanda, 64

Taliban (Afghanistan), 84
terrorism: Palestinians linked with,
76, 79
Thaci, Hashim, 50
Thailand, 16
Thucydides, 12
Timor Gap Oil Treaty (1989), 26
Tipton Three, 85
Tirman, John, 142–43n209
Tudjman, Franjo, 83
Turkey: Kurds in, 87–88
Tutsis: in Rwanda, 51, 52, 54, 55,
57, 59, 60, 66

Uganda, 20; under Amin, 150n266;
Congo invaded by, 66–67; S.
Rice on genocide in, 23;

Rwanda invaded by, 53–54, 63,
64
Ulmann, Richard H., 150n266
United Kingdom: American
colonists from, 10; Iraq bombed
by, 36; Iraqi sanctions and,
29–32
United Nations: on Congo, 67–68;
on Darfur Wars, 40–43, 107; on
Indonesian invasion of East
Timor, 89, 90; on invasion and
occupation of Iraq, 36–37; Iraqi
sanctions by, 29–31; on Israeli
invasion of Gaza Strip, 74, 76;
on "Responsibility to Protect,"
11–12, 20, 25–27, 115–16n19;
on Rwanda, 53, 56, 63–64; on
Sabra-Shatila massacre, 73
United Nations Commission on
the Truth for El Salvador, 91
United Nations Environmental
Program: on Darfur, 42; on
Gaza Strip, 77–78
United Nations High
Commissioner for Refugees
(UNHCR): on Rwanda, 57
United Nations Human Rights
Council, 74, 139n174; on Gaza
Strip, 76; Goldstone
Commission of, 77–80
United States: Central America
and, 91–94; colonial, 10; Dasht-
e-Leili massacre and, 84, 85;
extermination of Native
Americans in, 8–9; genocide
policy of, 23; Indonesian inva-
sion of East Timor and, 89;
International Court of Justice
and, 110; investigation of war
crimes committed by, 107–9;
Iraq invaded and occupied by,

33–38; Iraqi sanctions and, 29–32; Iraq policy of, 24–25; on Israeli invasion of Gaza Strip, 74–75, 80; Israel supported by, 69; military interventions by, 15–16; Operation Storm sponsored by, 83; post-World War II, 13–15; Rwanda and, 53–56, 60, 61, 63–64, 129–30n109; in Vietnam War, 19–20

Vietnam, 15–20
von Sponeck, Hans, 30–31

Walker, William, 96–100, 145n232
Wall Street Journal, 92
Warren, Rick, 20
Washington, George, 8
Washington Connection and Third World Fascism, The (Chomsky and Herman), 17

Washington Post, 81, 95
Webster, Daniel, 12
Weeks, William Earl, 8
Weller, Marc, 98
Western Slavonia, 82
Winthrop, John, 10
World Court, 11

Yaron, Amos, 71
Yugoslavia: Bosnia and Herzegovina in, 46–48; Croatia in, 81–83; International Court of Justice and, 110; international tribunals for, 21; Kosovo in, 49–51; Račak in, 95–101

Zaire. See Congo, Democratic Republic of
Zepa (Croatia), 82

CPSIA information can be obtained at www.ICGtesting.com
Printed in the USA
BVOW030555061212

307377BV00001B/3/P